National Museum

Publishers: George A. Christopoulos, John C. Bastias
Translation: Brian de Jongh
Managing Editor: E. Karpodini-Dimitriadi
Special Photography: Spyros Tsavdaroglou, Makis Skiadaresis, Nikos Kontos
Colour separation: Pietro Carlotti

National Museum

MANOLIS ANDRONICOS
Professor of Archaeology at the University of Thessalonike

EKDOTIKE ATHENON S.A.
Athens 1996

ISBN 960-213-025-3

Copyright © 1976
by
EKDOTIKE ATHENON S.A.
1, Vissarionos Street
Athens 106 72, Greece

PRINTED AND BOUND IN GREECE
BY
EKDOTIKE HELLADOS S.A.
An affiliated company
8, Philadelphias Street, Athens

History of the Museum

The National Archaeological Museum celebrates its first centenary in the course of this year (1974). As a result of a generous donation made by Demetrios Bernardakis the construction of the building was begun in 1866 on a plot of land presented by Helen Tositsa. The plans were drawn up by the architect Ludwig Lange. In 1874 the Greek state provided financial aid for the completion of the west wing to which the exhibits, until then housed in the Theseum, the Varvakeion and the Stoa of Hadrian, were removed. All the various collections belonged officially to the Central Archaeological Museum, which was founded by a royal decree of 13th November 1834 and whose headquarters were situated in the Theseum. The original name was officially preserved until 1888, when, by a royal decree of 19th April, it was changed to the National Archaeological Museum. Construction work continued and was finally completed in 1889. Lange's original design for the main façade, east wing and central hall was modified by the well-known architect, Ernst Ziller. The capital was thus embellished by another fine neo-Classical building and the country acquired its first large imposing museum. Various antiquities scattered about in different buildings in Athens were removed to the museum in 1891. Panayiotis Kavvadias, then general superintendent of Antiquities, placed the sculptures in the new halls and drafted the first catalogue. Christos Tsountas, the eminent Greek archaeologist, assembled the magnificent Mycenaean collection consisting of Schliemann's finds from the acropolis of Mycenae which he had recently excavated, and compiled the valuable index. The need to expand became imperative by 1925, and the construction of a new wing was begun. The new halls were completed in 1939. At the beginning of the Second World War, however, it was found necessary to close the museum, and bury the antiquities under ground in order to protect them from possible damage or destruction.

As soon as the war was over the prolonged and laborious task of uncovering the buried objects began. It was not only a case of cleaning and restoring them. The halls in which they were to be displayed were themselves in need of restoration. The fact that an initial temporary exhibition should have been organised in three halls of the Museum as early as 1946 was a remarkable achievement. More and more halls were opened at an ever-increasing speed, and both scholarly erudition and impeccable good taste were shown in the arrangement of the various collections. Many men and women made invaluable contributions, but it was Christos Karouzos' enlightened personality and indefatigable patience that constituted the driving force in initiating, supervising and accomplishing the laborious task. No marble memorial has yet been raised to his memory in the entrance way to the museum, but his spirit still roams the halls which he restored to life, rejoicing at the sight of the most beautiful sculptures.

The number of sculptures is staggering. Every site in the ancient Greek world, every period of ancient history, is represented. The epithet "National", as applied to the Museum, could not be more apt. It epitomizes the true character of its contents. For this is the only archaeological museum in the world in which so many masterpieces of ancient art have been assembled, in which it is possible for the visitor to follow the history of Greek art in all its manifestations, in an unbroken sequence from its genesis in the Neolithic age to its final swan song in the Roman period. In spite of the enormous quantity of exhibits it is not difficult to distinguish the basically most important collections. Scholarly specialists and lovers of art alike will be able to form a lucid and coherent picture of Greek art and its originality of form. The manner in which the exhibits have been arranged was not fortuitously arrived at; it was actually conceived with a view to facilitating the visitor's progress through the various halls. The first distinction to be made is between the four Prehistoric collections: those of Thessaly, the Cyclades, Thera and Mycenae. These serve as an excellent introduction to the principal works in the Museum: the works of art of the historical era, which are represented in the two main branches of sculpture and vase-painting. The various categories of the minor arts, ranging from coins and bronze idols to the products of the goldsmith's craft, are similarly dealt with. But among all these collections, it is one and one only that gives the National Archaeological Museum its special character: namely, the collection of incomparable monumental sculptures. For it was in the art of sculpture that the ancient Greeks excelled themselves more than any other people, either before or after them.

The Neolithic and Helladic civilizations

The first civilization to grow in Greece was the Neolithic; and the most important Neolithic sites have been identified in Thessaly. When Christos Tsountas, a pioneer in Prehistoric archaeology, started to excavate the two settlements of Dimeni and Sesklo near Volos, he opened the first chapter in the history of Greek civilization. The unexpectedly rich finds he brought to light in the course of these excavations were only a forecast of the undreamed of harvest of future archaeological research. At the beginning of the present century, there were no museums in those then remote parts of the country fit to house the important objects discovered in those exploratory excavations of Prehistoric sites. That is why Tsountas had them removed to the National Archaeological Museum, where they still remain, truncated, as it were, from the main body of finds, subsequently discovered, which now enrich the museum at Volos. Visitors to the National Archaeological Museum will consequently obtain their first glimpse of the dawn of Greek civilization in the clay idols and pottery of Neolithic Thessaly. And although idols may be no more than sculptural objects of the most primitive character, their robust composition, which is strikingly expressionistic, and the rough quality of their execution does not mean that they are devoid of any artistic or spiritual content. In their sharp clear-cut forms, their full sometimes outsize volumes and the abundance of their motifs, they not only possess a deep and many-faceted religious symbolism; they also reflect the basic social and economic differentiations which existed in the first permanent argicultural societies of the Neolithic settlements. The *kourotrophos,* the woman holding a child (fig. 2), found at Sesklo, is depicted enthroned; she is relatively richly adorned; and she has obviously climbed higher up the social ladder than those wide-hipped female figures of the earlier Neolithic age which are found in Thessaly and other parts of Greece (fig. 1). The intricate plasticity and architectural quality of a large idol (50 cm. in height) representing a seated male figure completes the picture, in so far as it illustrates the fact that religious and social requirements reflected in these works derive their source from relatively fairly developed levels of human existence.

Conclusive evidence is found in the Neolithic vases. The clean outlines and flowing curves of the earlier examples (fig. 4) are superceded by the more elaborate forms of the vases of the Middle Neolithic period with their simple though accurately conceived and carefully elaborated decoration. In the Late Neolithic period these are replaced by volumes and decorative work of an unexpected dynamic quality (fig. 3), with complicated designs and colours and an intricacy of composition which raises the question whether aesthetic feeling has mastered the calculated disposition of forms or whether the potter, in his wisdom, has succeeded, within the limits of the geometric motifs at his disposal, to harp back to some rich and ancestral world and thus transcend his purely instinctive sensibility as an artist.

In this hall the visitor may cast a brief glance at the elegant Early Helladic "sauce-boats" with their delicately curved spouts before proceeding to look at the austere Minyan vases with their resemblance to metal vessels and the opaque decoration of the matt-painted vases which archaeologists ascribe to the Middle Helladic period and which are probably the artistic creations of the first Hellenic tribes.

Cycladic civilization

If variety is the hallmark of Greek civilization, the different currents discernible in its earliest stages may be likened to rivulets gushing out of innumerable springs flowing in different directions, converging and diverging, until they finally unite into the larger stream in order to pour into and swell the waters of the main river. While continental Greece continued to follow its own course, renovating the road initially opened by its Neolithic inhabitants, the Cyclades, scattered all over the Central Aegean, rendered prosperous by their trade in a recently discovered metal (namely, copper), entered the scene with a flourish in the 3rd millennium B.C. Once again we must recall the achievement of Christos Tsountas, who was the first archaeologist to uncover and present in the late 19th century the remarkable remains of the Cycladic civilization. The atmosphere of the Cyclades is distinguished by the refractory light that emanates from the marble strata of the soil. This white stone, which is one of the chief glories of Greece, was extensively quarried in the Cycladic archipelago. Crystalline in texture, lacking the hard quality of

GROUND PLAN OF THE MAIN FLOOR OF
THE NATIONAL ARCHAEOLOGICAL MUSEUM

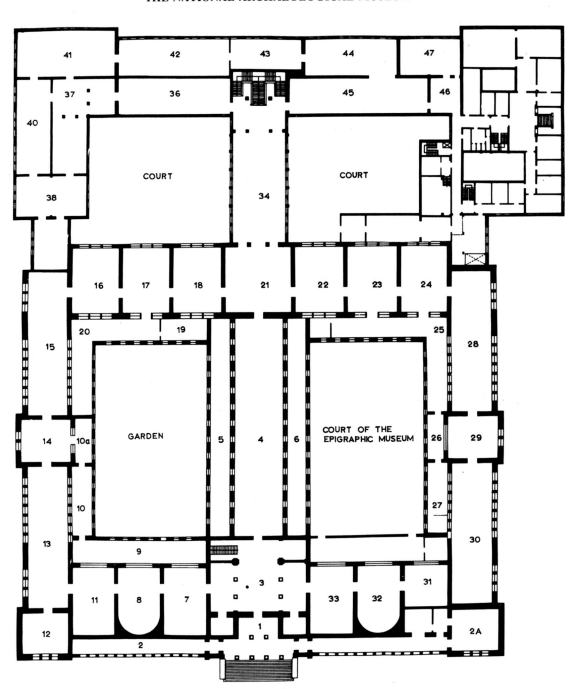

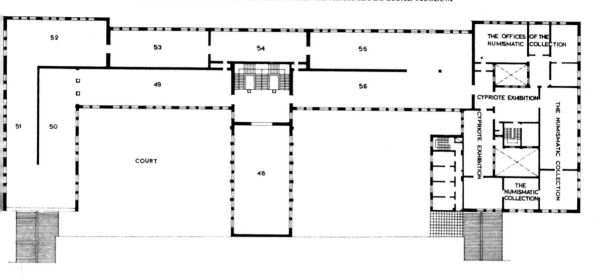

Plan of the main floor of the National Archaelolgical Museum

1. Porch 2. Northern stoa 2A..Exhibition of mouldings 3. Entrance Hall 4. Mycenaean room 5. Neolithic and premycenaean room 6. Cycladic room 7. 1st room of archaic sculpture 8.2nd room of archaic sculpture 9-10A.Small rooms of archaic works 11. 3rd room of archaic sculpture 12. 4th room of archaic sculpture 13. Room of Aristodikos 14. Room containing early classical *stelai* (Gravestones) 15. Room of Poseidon 16. 1st room of classical grave stelai 17. Room of classical votive reliefs 18. 2nd room of classical grave reliefs 19-20. Two small rooms of classical works 21. Room of the Diadoumenos 22. Room of Epidauros 23. 1st room of grave stelai of the 4th century B.C. 24. 2nd room of grave monuments of the 4th century B.C. 25. Two rooms of decree and votive reliefs 26. 3rd small room of votive reliefs 27. 4th small room of votive reliefs 28. Grave monuments of the 4th century B.C. Room of the Youth from Antikythera 29. Room of Thémis. 30. Room of Hellenistic sculpture 31. Temporary exhibits 32. Stathatos Collection 34. Room of the Altar 35. Staircase to the 1st floor. 36. Carapanos Collection 37. Bronze room 38-40. Rooms closed 41-43. Rooms containing works from the roman period 44, 46, 47. Rooms closed 45. 2nd Bronze room.

Plan of the 1st floor

48. The Thera frescoes 49. Room of geometrio vases 50. Room of geometric vases from different workshops 51. Room of Vari vases 52. Room of Heraeum of Argos and Sophilos 53. Room of black - figure vases 54. Room of black - figure and red - figure vases 55. Room of white - ground lekythoi - red - figure vases - Choe 56. Room of vases of the 4th century B.C. Room of Epinetron of Eretria.

the stone which craftsmen elsewhere found so difficult to work, marble enabled Cycladic artists to exploit the possibilities of the material at hand with excellent results. Marble vases with daring and elegant forms reveal the artists' skill and the high standard of civilization reached by the people who made use of them. But the sphere in which Cycladic artists excelled themselves was in that of sculptured idols. Innumerable marble idols depict the figure of a nude woman with her hands placed across her stomach. Only the breasts and nose are plastically rendered; other features, such as the mouth and eyes, were most probably painted. The little idols must have been immensely popular, for great quantities have been found, not only in the Cyclades themselves, but in the more remote parts of continental and insular Greece. The significance of the idols in the context of the history of art might have been a limited one, had the artists simply confined themselves to rendering this enigmatic female figure (Mother Earth?) in the form of a small-scale object. But the more talented and inspired artists seem, on occasion, to have had the opportunity to create much larger idols, distinguished for their admirable sculptural finish. The large almost life-size idol from Amorgos (fig. 7) is a masterpiece of large sculpture. The sculptor seems to have been particularly daring in rendering the general form and, more important, in providing the plastic levels of the human body with animation. The clarity of the figure and the vibratory quality of the marble surfaces are likely to draw the attention of experts in modern abstract art. Henry Moore, greatest of living sculptors, was intensely moved when he first saw it, lying, as it then was, in a case in the Museum. Besides possessing both skill and sensitivity, Cycladic artists had acquired an intelligent conception of volumes. The remarkable idol of a harpist is an outstanding example (fig. 5). Notice the rhythmical intricacy of the modelling and the special function of the curve followed in the movement of the members of the body and of the harp itself. The architectural modelling vies with the delicate finish applied to the marble surface. It also confirms the fact that the simpler but no less charming and intelligent rendering of a flute-player depicted in another idol (fig. 6), was not purely fortuitous, but a happy combination of artistic sensibility, long experience and patient labour. A similar painstaking feeling for decoration is observed in the strange clay utensils shaped like frying-pans (fig. 8), whose function remains an enigma and which were found lying in tombs beside the idols. The clay surface is incised with tangent spirals, star-shaped decorative designs, and even representations of ships, all of which are executed with the accuracy and sensitivity associated with a true feeling for aesthetic expression and the existence of an evolved social structure.

The Thera frescoes

At one time a number of archaeologists believed that the decline of Cycladic civilization had set in by the end of the 3rd millennium B.C. More recent archaeological excavations, however, have brought to light important remains which indicate that the end of the millennium was not characterized so much by decline as by a complete transformation wrought by the expansion of the Minoan maritime empire of the New Palace period (c. 1600 B.C.). Fragments of frescoes and vase-paintings excavated at Phylakopi on the island of Melos do not merely stress the fact that the influence exercised by Minoan civilization undoubtedly prevailed throughout the Eastern Mediterranean; they go much farther, enabling us to envisage a Cretan colonization and domination of the Aegean islands, especially of the most southerly ones. This argument could not have been so effectively supported but for the recent excavations at Kea and, above all, the astonishing discoveries made by Professor Marinatos at Thera. The Thera exhibits, now displayed in the halls of the National Archaeological Museum, consist, among other objects, of frescoes which are among the most striking in the whole of Minoan painting. The circumstances in which Thera was destroyed by a tremendous volcanic eruption account for the fact that large sections of the frescoes have survived in such a good state of preservation. A systematic method of excavation has also contributed greatly to their undamaged condition and to the possibility of their admirable restoration.

The first frescoes to be uncovered and restored revealed an art, at once so lavish and so full of charm, that they clearly seemed to be the works of the most skilled and inspired painters of Minoan Crete. They also supplied evidence of the existence on the island of a city, whose economic, social and cultural evolution bore comparison with those of the most important centres of Minoan civilization. Among the most remarkable features of the fresco of the Spring (fig. 14) are the harmonious deep-toned colours of the rocks, and the delicacy of the slender leaf-stalks of lilies which terminate in innumerable purple-petalled flowers, like little tongues of flame of the utmost elegance and fragility of form. Swallows flutter among the flowers in a state of celestial intoxication: sometimes in couples, their bills half-open, as they pursue their erotic games in the perfumed air. It is like a paean to nature, a hymn of joy and hope. A fresco of this kind could only have been conceived in a society which, knowing the meaning of true felicity, dwelt, under an azure sky, on the wave-lashed island of Santorine, "queen of the earth's vibrations and of the flutter of Aegean wings", as the poet O. Elytis says.

The lyrical quality of this fresco borders on the unique. But for sheer sensibility, gaiety and lightness of touch, reflecting a love and knowledge of everyday life, the fresco of the Boxing Children is even more impressive (fig. 10). It portrays two children with exquisite eyes and long wavy locks. Their expressions possess a disarming seriousness. Wearing nothing but a loin-cloth, their limbs burned by the sun, they stand erect, with clenched fists and an air of anticipation that suggests they are about to deal the first blows of a harsh sport which is transformed here into the noblest and most innocent of games. Beside the fresco of the Boxing Children is that of a nude fisherman (fig. 11), which provides further proof of the high standard of artistic ability of the Minoan painters of Thera. A typical Aegean figure, at once familiar, lively and warm-hearted, he holds his catch of fish in both hands in a relaxed yet purposeful attitude.

There are also depictions of nimble antelopes (fig. 12), rendered with well-judged simplicity and accurately calculated contours, and fragments of other figures, such as those of the Blue Monkeys. It would appear that we now have a fairly complete picture of Minoan painting in Thera. But no. The picture would not be absolutely complete. It would not do full justice to the accomplishments and capabilities of these painters, had not the fresco of the Ships been uncovered and restored. This astonishing work was discovered in the West House, one of whose walls was decorated with the fresco of the Fisherman. It consists of an oblong frieze (six metres are preserved lengthwise) in which a series of crowded "historical" events are depicted in miniature painting. The archaeologist who uncovered it believes that the scene represents the events of a naval campaign rendered in a sequence not unlike that of a film unfolding on a cinema screen.

Mycenaean civilization

At approximately the same period, that is to say, in the 16th century B.C., the first powerful dynasties were establishing their authority over the great citadels of mainland Greece. First, and most important of all, was Mycenae, which acquired an even greater glory in the ancient world than Athens itself. The opening Mycenaean chapter begins with a flourish, for its kings founded a dynasty whose legendary celebrity not only outlived antiquity but remains alive to this day. When Agamemnon, the most famous descendant of these kings, decided to wage a campaign against Troy, he united the whole Greek world: a world known as Mycenaean because of the fame of Agamemnon's capital. It remained for Homer to immortalize this war in world literature as none other ever has been, either before or after. The memory of the legendary city, Homer's "rich-in-gold Mycenae", remained alive in the imagination of the ancient Greeks just as the memory of Constantinople survived in the dreams of later generations of Greeks. In 1876, when Heinrich Schliemann excavated the royal shaft graves of Mycenae and found them filled with priceless treasures, he laid the foundations of Mycenaean archaeology. The introductory chapter in the history of the first Greeks who came here in the beginning of the 2nd millennium B.C. was thus opened. The precious objects discovered in the graves were removed to the National Archaeological Museum to form the first Mycenaean collection, which is being constantly enriched by new finds.

The large well-lit hall facing the monumental entrance contains crowded groups of objects characteristic of a civilization which possessed an almost embarrassingly exaggerated feeling for power and wealth. The show-cases are filled with objects wrought in gold and ivory. The clay vases, large and of infinite variety, do not detract from the prevailing sense of unity. Both the materials employed and the forms given to these works of art would appear strange to a Greek of the Classical age. From the outset it is clear that all these valuable objects — vases, weapons, architectural fragments and works of the minor arts — are the expression of an attitude towards life that differs wholly from that of the Greeks of the historical era. Their chief characteristic, one might say, is *élan vital*. The vegetation is pliant; flowing lines characterize the plants; nature is wild and untamed, populated by felines; the forces of nature are presented in their most elemental ungovernable form. The bull, the octopus, the lion and its hunters, the trees thick with leafy branches and the slender plants with flowers, all combine to present an image of an elegiac existence in which man, rejoicing in his freedom, moves impulsively and embraces the world with uncontrollable vitality. There can be no doubt that the art of Minoan Crete exercised an enormous influence on the creative forms of expression of the Mycenaeans. But the inner core of the Mycenaean world is a wholly indigenous one. Compared with the Minoans, the Mycenaeans emerge as a more robust people, possessed of a more dynamic vision. They delight in the creation of more vigorous sturdier forms. It is the harsh reality of ceaseless struggle, not the joys of pleasurable dalliance that motivate the impulsive actions of these figures. Among all these forceful shifting shapes it is not impossible to discern a firmer structure destined to develop and, with the passage of time, lead to the more rational rhythm and architectural composition of Greek form.

The treasures of the royal shaft graves

Schliemann, who possessed a boundless imagination, was always an inveterate enthusiast. He believed the gold mask found in the fifth grave of the inner Grave Circle of the Mycenaean acropolis to have been that of Agamemnon, and to have somehow reproduced the actual facial features of the mythical king (fig. 17). But neither this mask, nor the other four that have survived, are likely to be faithful reproductions of the actual faces they once covered. It is even less likely that they can be identified with specific individuals. But the pale sheen of gold and the different features rendered on each of the masks conjures up a vision of the chill hand of death that has lain so long on the faces of the ancient rulers of Mycenae. "Emptiness... below the buried gold mask", as G. Seferis says. All around the masks lay the gold chest ornaments, the gold diadems (fig. 15), the heavy costly swords and finely wrought daggers with inlaid decoration and lavish handles (figs. 22-26), as well as all kinds of vases executed in gold and silver. Although this impressive, but never barbaric, display of wealth, these costly raw materials moulded into forms and shapes with matchless technical skill and genuine artistic inspiration combine to provide a picture of a strong thoroughly disciplined military organization, the feeling for cultural development, the love of art and beauty for its own sake is never absent. Every object may be worthy of note, but particular attention should be paid to certain works of the minor arts of the early Mycenaean period. First, the rhyton (libation vessel), in the shape of a bull's head (fig. 20), fashioned out of silver, with horns of gold and a gold rosette on the forehead. An impression of the awesome but sacred animal's nature is successfully conveyed by the carefully calculated volumes. Another rhyton, in the shape of a lion's head (fig. 21), made of gold, forms a striking counterpart to the bull's head. But the disposition of the volumes in this example is more austere and geometrical; there is a different feeling — more tectonic, one might almost say, more native, more Greek — which is particularly evident in the sharply defined edge of the surfaces and in the rendering of details.

The Vapheio cups

The finest works of art wrought in embossed gold were not found in the royal shaft graves of Mycenae, but in a *tholos* tomb near ancient Amyklai. These superb objects are the two so-called Vapheio Cups dated to the late 16th or early 15th century B.C. (figs. 18-19). A turbulent scene of the capture of a bull in a net is depicted on one cup; on the other we have a serene picture of shepherds accompanied by their cattle. These two works are unique, not only because of their creator's technical skill; the sensitivity of his approach to his theme, combined with the admirable composition, the power of expression and well-calculated filling up of the spaces raise his work to the highest level of artistic achievement.

Gravestones

Among the wealth of objects discovered in the royal shaft graves the gravestones occupy a special place, because they are the earliest specimens of large-scale Greek sculpture in relief. They consequently play an extremely important role in the history not only of Mycenaean but of the whole of Greek art. The representations of chariots and beasts are well judged, but the execution is inferior to that of contemporary works of the minor arts. The geometric decoration, which consists of spirals however, is composed and incised with such an assurance and feeling for decorative embellishment that the gravestones may unreservedly be classed as works of high quality. More important, they are creations of manifestly Mycenaean origin, firmly rooted in indigenous elements, which survived in the midst of an attractive world of Minoan influences, only to blossom forth in their pure form in the historical era, well after the final dissolution of the Mycenaean world.

Works of art wholly representative of that Mycenaean world which dominated Greece for more than four hundred years are not only found in the astonishing yield of the royal shaft graves. Specimens of frescoes with strong Minoan influences have been uncovered in a very fragmentary condition in the Mycenaean palaces of the last phase of the period. In 1970 Professor G. Mylonas discovered and restored part of a fresco showing a female figure which he called the Mycenaean Woman (fig. 31). The facial features, together with the artistic expression, with its strong Mycenaean character, its bold and revolutionary originality, distinguish this attractive lady from the numerous female figures of the Minoan frescoes. Unlike the Minoan figures, the Mycenaean Woman is no longer depicted in profile. The figure stands frontally, in an attitude of exquisite nobility. Only the head is turned sideways, enabling the onlooker to obtain a view of the delicate profile. The arms are animated by harmonious movements. A third dimension is thus created for the first time in Greek art, and the feeling for space is admirably rendered.

Frescoes

The ivory objects of the minor arts (fig. 27), discovered both at Mycenae and in other parts of the country, should also be ascribed to the last phase of Mycenaean civilization. Among these a group depicting a small childlike figure between two larger female ones is worth noting (fig. 28). It has been suggested that it may be a representation of Demeter, Persephone and Iakchos. The idea is certainly an attractive one. But can it be proved? The religious faith of the Minoans and Mycenaeans is shrouded in obscurity. Not a single record has yet shed any light worthy of serious attention. We can only guess at the contents — not interpret them.

Vase-painting and sculpture

It is equally impossible to interpret the mysterious sculptured limestone head with deep blue eyes, eyebrows and hair, red lips and three dots on the cheeks and chin (fig. 29). Is it a depiction of a sphinx? Or the representation of some great goddess sculptured for the first time on such a large scale in the

Hellenic world? Identity apart, the head may nevertheless be considered to be the distant precursor of the Greek sculptures of the historical period.

Particular attention should be paid to the unique Warrior Vase (fig. 30), which is also a forerunner of things to come. Entirely foreign to the Minoan vase-painting tradition, which was assimilated into Mycenaean art, this superb krater has the quality of a symbolic representation of all the various elements of which the Mycenaean empire was composed. Heavily armed hoplites, complete with breast-plates, greaves, helmets, shields and spears march solemnly in single file. At the end of the procession a woman raises her hand in a gesture of farewell. It is as though the artist had caught the very essence of the moment, when the "bronze-clad Achaians" set out from home to engage the enemy in one of their famous campaigns. Only after many centuries shall we again see such a well-knit composition, such well-designed, well-set up figures in Greek vase-painting. The vision of this procession of marching men, contemporaries of the first great catastrophe that befell the Mycenaean world in *c*. 1200 B.C., haunts the imagination. The warriors themselves were destined to perish in the ruins of Mycenae. It remained only for the great rhapsodist of the Geometric period — for Homer himself — to restore them to life in his immortal epic.

The end of the Mycenaean era

The end of the Mycenaean world left a deep mark on Greek history. Although we do not know what actually happened in the 12th century B.C. nor what was the cause of the destruction of the Mycenaean cities in *c*. 1200 B.C., followed by the end of Mycenaean civilization in *c*. 1100 B.C., we may be absolutely certain that a profound and radical historical change took place — but that it took place without completely sapping the roots of the old civilization. A study of the art of the centuries following the Mycenaean period, synoptically referred to as the Geometric age, leads to two important conclusions: (1) that the earlier forces were exhausted and replaced by new ones inspired by a primitive impetus and fresh dynamic quality; (2) that this new world was nevertheless no more than a continuity of the old one and its roots sprang from the same soil. The finest and most lavish creations of Geometric art, which originated in Attica, were ceramic products. During four centuries — from the 11th to the 8th — the potters' workshops in Athens evolved an unparalleled tradition in the art of ceramics and vase-painting that suffered no break in continuity and laid the firm foundations of all the admirable creations of succeeding centuries. A fundamental change had already occurred in vase decoration during the earliest phase of that period, the so-called Protogeometric phase (1050-900 B.C.). Pure geometric patterns, characterized by rythm, symmetry and precision, gave new vigour to art and offered artists new means of expression. This style displayed a novel structure and crystalline purity, features that were unknown, or rather lost, in the prolific diversity of the natural forms of Creto-Mycenaean art. An even more radical change than the one observed in decorative work occurred in the architectural solidity acquired by the vases. The flexibility and extreme tension of the Minoan forms had, in the course of the development of Mycenaean pottery, lost the vital force of the initial creation and gave the impression of a certain lack of firmness. The forms, now purged of these earlier elements, acquired a new plastic purity which proved a determining factor in the genesis of genuine Greek art. It is as though the Greek races, freed themselves of the spell of the Minoan world, and returned once more to the sobriety of the Middle Helladic age.

Geometric art

Nowhere can the progressive development of the early stages in the art of ceramics be more usefully examined than in the National Archaeological Museum. The first Protogeometric specimens consist of relatively small vases. There is little variety in shape, and they are very simply and soberly decorated with concentric circles and plain meander patterns. Development in the sphere of geometric abstract forms may be slow, but it is organic. In time the simple rhythmical lines are transformed into lavish and varied decorative motifs. The forms of the vases acquire a greater sensitivity and the contours become increasingly calculated and opulent; the inherent simplicity of a vase does not handicap the potter's imagination; he creates new forms, new variations on old themes. In the field of decorative work, the artist's imagination vies with his skill, his sensitivity with his long-acquired knowledge. The lavish decoration created by means of the repetition and elaboration of straight lines in a series of impressive compositions is astonishing. At first the artist reserves two or three unpainted bands on the dark surface of the vase: on the belly, neck and base. On these he then adds a motif which is developed by means of repetition all round the vase. Gradually, the bands increase in number, covering the vessel's entire surface which is thus rendered increasingly brighter. At the beginning of the 8th century B.C. the surface is covered with bands of unequal height decorated with geometric motifs. A special role is reserved for the meander pattern, both in its simplest and most intricate forms. This motif, which is full of momentum and possesses an incalculable dynamic quality and capacity for infinite development, both as regards height and width, acquired numerous variations in Greek — particularly Attic — art and was transformed from a formal ornament into a flexible dynamic feature.

In the process of evolving geometric decoration Attic artists laid down the first principles of representational painting which were inherited and fully developed by future generations. Limited representations of animals and scenes of everyday life were initially painted in a confined space within the area reserved for abstract designs. These representations quickly increased in number and during the last phase of the Geometric period (750-700 B.C.) they tempered the severity of the decorative system, thus opening the way for the radical changes effected in the early 7th century B.C. Furthermore, an exceptional opportunity to carry out these changes lay in the fact that the Athenians were in the habit of placing vases on tombs. The bottom of the vase was drilled in order that libations for the dead might be poured into the vessel. At first small and insignificant, they gradually acquired monumental size, up to a height of one or even one and a half metres. These large vases, amphoras and kraters (figs. 32-33), no longer executed in order to serve a purely functional purpose, were thus raised to an altogether higher level of art. The larger dimensions, the structure and organization combined to produce not only an outstanding creation of the potter's art but also an architectural and sculptural form. On these vases artists of the Geometric period depicted funerary scenes, such as the lying-in-state of the dead, the funeral procession, chariot processions and representations of ships. Some of the representations are perhaps related to mythical events. It was at this point that vase-painters certainly began to draw inspiration from mythology. Another precious contribution was thus made to Greek art. As one follows the course of Geometric pottery in the objects displayed in the show-cases of the National Museum and is finally confronted with the imposing funerary vases which rise up like genuine statues, one cannot fail to be moved by an art capable of creating masterpieces out of such a common material as clay.

Assimilation of Oriental influences

Towards the end of the 8th century B.C. another profound change took place in the Greek world, and the new currents were strongly reflected in the sphere of art. During the first half of the 7th century B.C. Oriental influences affected artistic forms to the extent that the period came to be known as the "Orientalizing" one. Ceramics too were not unaffected by the new ideas. An unusual situation, which will continue to be discerned throughout the history of Greek art, arose; and we are thus able to distinguish two contradictory elements: on the one hand, a tendency for innovation; on the other, a tenacious attachment to tradition. Greek artists were always open-minded, always ready to exploit anything gained from their contacts with foreign or associated civilizations. At the same time they preserved and developed all the finest elements they had inherited from their own art and civilization. Old forms were thus fertilised by new ideas, and rejuvenated by foreign formal features. It is consequently more accurate to speak of Hellenization of Oriental influences than of an "Orientalizing" Greek art.

The best example is found in the Protoattic vases, as those produced in Attica at the time (700-630 B.C.) were called. The exotic plants and animals of the Orient were now included in the decoration of the large Protoattic vases — but their role was a subordinate one. Human figures, horses and processions of chariots — subjects established by Geometric tradition — still occupy the chief place in vase decoration. Their forms, however, acquire a new substance and therefore a new content, because the changes wrought by Oriental influences on Attic art had the effect of rejuvenating the essential nature of the form rather than of enriching it with borrowed foreign themes. This rejuvenated form reflected the essence of the Greek world in its most profound sense, expressing it in terms of mythology. The number of painted themes derived from mythology expanded at an ever-increasing rate. Mythology became a limitless source from which artists drew their inspiration, and for the first time the myths themselves were provided with eloquent and tangible forms. The fact cannot be sufficiently stressed that contemporary artists were now emboldened to provide the shapeless visages of the gods and heroes of whom the poets had sung with positive forms.

The fragile shapes of Cycladic vases, notable for their pronounced Oriental influences, their less austere structure and their creators' greater love of picturesque and pictorial detail, which now stand beside the Protoattic examples in the halls of the National Archaeological Museum, are like an echo from an early Archaic island world. Two large amphorae (both about one metre high) from Delos are outstanding examples of the standard of workmanship attained by a Cycladic workshop after 650 B.C. These vases used to be called "Melian": an epithet now considered to be certainly incorrect. It is more commonly believed that the vases were products of some other island, possibly Paros. One of the vases is decorated with a magnificent representation of Apollo riding a chariot drawn by winged horses, followed by the two Hyperborean virgins and led by Artemis (fig. 34). On the other, Herakles is depicted bidding farewell to the parents of his bride who is already mounted on his chariot.

Black-figure vases

The life span of the other potters' workshops, each of which possessed its own individuality, its own list of achievements, was of shorter duration. One might almost say that they served as a complement to the great Attic workshops whose productivity was seemingly inexhaustible. The creative range and rejuvenating force of the Attic potter remain unique. The act of creation was accompanied by the acquisition of experience and the assimilation of the technical accomplishments of other schools. During the 7th century B.C. Corinth was the greatest centre of productivity and Corinthian workshops had soon captured all the markets in the East and West. Corinthian potters seem to have specialized in small-scale vases, the decoration of which possessed a singular precision and crystalline clarity, as well as sensitivity of feeling. These miniature Corinthian compositions are a unique achievement in Greek art. And it was precisely because of the small dimensions of their vases that the Corinthians were obliged to develop faultless technical methods in order to achieve in miniature what other craftsmen were accomplishing in the field of large-scale pottery. The technique of the black-figure vase was a Corinthian achievement. A superb technique designed to reflect the atmosphere of the early Archaic world was achieved by means of filling in the figures with black paint, of registering details with precision and extremely carefully executed incisions, and using a deep reddish-violet paint which provided richness of colour without harming the unit of the decoration.

Attic artists were quick to learn the lesson from their Corinthian colleagues. Cautiously, somewhat hesitantly at first, then more boldly, they sought to adapt the perfection of the black-figure technique to their own more inspired vision. By the end of the 7th century B.C. Attic artists were thus producing their own black-figure vases. If the Piraeus amphora, on which a magnificent cock is depicted on the neck and a procession of chariots on the body, is the earliest example of this style, the first great vase-painter must be the one known as the "Nessos painter", because he executed the amphora in the National Archaeological Museum in which Herakles and the centaur Nessos are depicted on the neck and the legend of Perseus and Medusa on the belly (fig. 35). A new world is now reflected in the forms and paintings of the vases. A new structure, severe and solid, yet opulent and dynamic, shapes the body of the vase and its various parts. In the sphere of vase-painting a new world, at once vigorous and majestic, is peopled by mighty heroes and "terrible monsters". The lions and wild beasts of the east have acquired a Greek sturdiness as well as a different content. Almost the entire work of the great Attic artist who painted this new vision of the world may be seen in the National Archaeological Museum, because Attica had not yet captured the foreign markets, and most of the Attic products thus remained at home, where they were eventually found centuries later.

By the beginning of the 6th century B.C., the charm of the black-figure vases had begun to make its impact abroad and the finest products were exported to wealthy foreign commercial centres, chiefly in Italy. The Tyrrhenians, as well as the Greeks of Magna Graecia, collected Attic masterpieces in the 6th and 5th centuries B.C. and placed them on well constructed tombs as offerings to the dead. It was therefore from these tombs that Europe subsequently acquired its knowledge of Greek vases. Priceless collections were assembled from the treasure-house of antiquity and eventually found their way to the Vatican, the Louvre, the British Museum and other great museums of the world. Consequently, the National Archaeological Museum's collection of 6th and 5th century B.C. pottery cannot compare with some of those now in foreign museums. The National Archaeological Museum has, nevertheless, quite a great deal to offer, both to the scholar and the enthusiastic amateur, in the way of ceramics which were produced in such abundance during the 6th and 5th centuries B.C. All the vases are characterized by perfection of form and an infinite variety of decorative themes drawn from Greek mythology. Some of the show-cases contain fragments of vases that littered the Athenian Acropolis: all that survived the Persian holocaust. These may not attract much attention; nor are any of the compositions intact. But the excellence of design, the elegant incisions and the technical experience of the artists are clearly apparent. Among these are the sherds with the inscription "Sophilos painted me". For the first time, we thus learn the name of an Athenian vase-painter (c. 580 B.C.). It is only on the sherds, too, that we read the inscription "Lydos painted me", and learn the name of one of the greatest artists of the 6th century B.C. The name of another equally gifted contemporary artist, who executed the magnificent *dinos*, which was found on the Acropolis and established him as the "painter of the Acropolis 606", is unfortunately nowhere to be found. The cauldron-shaped vase is covered with decorative representations. A mythical combat, in which a fine array of chariots take part, is depicted on the main band. Sir John Beazley, an outstanding expert on Greek vase-painting, says: "This is at last a picture that for size, grandeur and vehemence may rank with the masterpieces of the 'Nessos painter' and his colleagues". "Its merits", he adds, "make this one of the best battle-pieces in Archaic art". Magnificent examples of black-figure painting are to be found in some of the flat rectangular plaques on which funerary scenes were depicted. These would appear to have constituted the decoration reserved for sepulchral memorials raised above ground. Evidence of the importance attached by the family of the deceased to this form of decoration lies in the fact that the plaques in the National Archaeological Museum are the works of Lydos, whom we have already mentioned, and of Exekias, the great black-figure vase-painter — perhaps the greatest of all Attic vase-painters — who executed a whole series of masterpieces over a period of three decades (550-520 B.C.).

A special category of black-figure vases is to be found in the so-called "Panathenaic amphoras" (fig. 43). These vessels, filled with oil from Athena's sacred olive trees, were presented as awards to victors in the Panathenaic games. They were first produced in 566 B.C. with the institution of the Panathenaic games and their production continued until the Roman period in the twilight years of antiquity. Evidence of the particular function for which they were destined is also found in their decoration: a depiction of Athena Promachos on one side, scenes of contests on the other. It was because of this function, which aimed at preserving the tradition of awarding first prizes, that vase-painters retained the Archaic technique of the black-figure style until the very end. The innovations so effectively introduced by the red-figure style were thus ignored by the painters of the "Panathenaic amphoras"

Red-figure vases

The workshop of Exekias was one of the busiest in Athens. There Exekias, both potter and vase-painter, fashioned vases of new attractive shapes and painted them in his own incomparable manner. The artist known as the "Andokides painter", who had the brilliant inspiration to reverse the chromatic relation between the figures and the surface of the vase and thus create the red-figure style, seems to have served his apprenticeship in Exekias' work-shop. The figures in this new style no longer resemble black sketches on a red ground; in fact the ground acquires a black metallic glaze and the figures, which remain red and luminous, are thus provided with an unexpected corporality. New horizons were now opened up to Athenian vase-painters. Beyond them extended untrodden and alluring paths. No longer inhibited by the severe and limited capacities of the black-figure technique, draughtsmen were able to put their abilities to the test, enchanted by the infinite variety of theme execution at their disposal. The National Archaeological Museum does not possess fine works of such great craftsmen and innovators as Euthymides and Euphronios, the "Kleophrades painter" and the "Berlin painter", but it has a large number of less important works, which nevertheless illustrate the extent to which the art of the Classical period encompassed the entire range of human existence. Even the most modest works — seldom beyond the means of the humblest Athenian citizen — displayed a freshness of outlook and the achievements of art in that age.

Among the vases of this common category which were, for the most part, found in Attic tombs, where they had been placed as offerings to the dead, a fair number may be distinguished for their size and artistic merit. On them the name of some eminent artist is sometimes inscribed; on other occasions we may discern the seal of the artist's personality, the originality of whose design we have learnt to recognise from the audacious and unparalleled studies of the great expert, sir John Beazley. In a broken *kylix* of the late 6th century B.C. decorated with the subject of the wedding of Peleus and Thetis, always a great favourite with Attic vase-painters, we have the signature of the potter and painter, Euphronios. In another piece, which is intact, decorated with the representation of a kneeling warrior, we read the inscription "Phintias made me", which means that it was a work by the contemporary of Euphronios. In a third *kylix*, which is of a later date than the other two, a young man is depicted holding a *kylix* in his left hand, an *oinochoe* in his right, advancing towards an altar inscribed with the words "Oh, Douris!". Douris is known to have been one of the most able and prolific vase-painters of the early 5th century B.C. A superb *pelike* (a kind of amphora) is the work of a vase-painter, known as the "Pan painter", which he decorated with a representation of the combat between Herakles and Bousiris, a mythical king of Egypt (fig. 40). The dramatic force of this tumultuous composition, combined with its effortless humour and felicitous conception, is so judiciously adapted to the form of the vase as to fully justify the feeling of veneration that often overwhelms the visitor when contemplating the masterpieces of Attic vase-painting.

During the Classical period, Attic vase-painters, whose works were advancing on lines parallel to those of monumental sculpture, executed a series of masterpieces which are wholly remarkable for the elegance of draughtsmanship, the fullness of form and the sense of balance. The "Achilles painter", a contemporary of Pheidias, painted figures comparable to the noble youths of Pheidias' frieze and provided his entire composition with an architectural firmness that recalls the Parthenon sculptures. But dangers lay ahead. The works of large painting, now lost to us, exercised so great a fascination on vase-painters that, in so far as decoration was concerned, they inevitably went too far. The result was the execution of Attic works that went beyond the limits of Classical balance and, more important, exceeded the potential capacity of expression inherent in a vase-painting. The style known as the Beautiful Style soon became the Rich Style, which was characterized by extreme emphasis on draughtsmanship and compositional skill, together with an excessive exploitation of painting impressions spread carelessly over the surface of the vase, thus breaking up its aesthetic unity. Although the calligraphic and extremely fine treatment of old themes in the works of such notable artists as Polygnotos and the "Eretria painter", who executed the elegant Eretria *epinetron* (fig. 44) deserve respect, the dynamic force and expressive quality of the design of the earlier craftsmen are absent. Moreover, as the representations became increasingly covered with gaudy colours and designs which possessed no interior vitality and, more important, were devoid of any aesthetic justification, the fate of red-figure vase-painting was sealed. The end came in the 4th century B.C.

White-ground vases. White-ground lekythoi

In Athens of the 5th century B.C., the art of the vase-painter found, as the 19th century poet, Dionysios Solomos says, "its good and sweet hour". For some time artists were to experiment with yet another technique destined to produce a series of matchless masterpieces. The projection of light-coloured figures of the red-figure style on a black ground created a strong contrast with the sharp outlines and the isolation of the figures from their surroundings. By means of a new method, the entire surface of the vase, covered with a very fine white glaze, acquired cohesion. The figures were painted on the glaze, the hair and sometimes, the garments and other minor details being rendered in dark colours. The monotonous black colour too was now replaced by a variety of lighter shades. The composition thus acquired a more pictorial character and created a gentler and uniform atmosphere. Above all, the merits of the representation rested on perfection of design, quality of line and the painter's ability to render the plasticity and volumes of the figure solely by means of outlines. Among the earliest and finest examples of white-ground vases is the *kylix,* on which the murder of Orpheus by the Thracian women is depicted, by the so-called "Pistoxenos painter" (*c.* 470 B.C.). The few surviving fragments (the head of Orpheus, part of his lyre and a woman holding a double axe) are sufficient to enable us to observe the excellence of the work. The savage theme is rendered in the grand manner; the beautiful faces possess a deep spiritual quality and the "character" of the protagonists is expressed through the quality and purity of the design.

This technique was particularly well suited to a type of vase known as the white *lekythos* which was intended to accompany the dead on their journey into eternity. The National Archaeological Museum possesses the largest collection of white-ground *lekythoi* which are displayed in a hall almost entirely reserved for them. The subject-matter of the representations is invariably associated with the deceased. If one may borrow a musical metaphor, one might describe them as "variations on a theme". The *lekythoi* require the closest possible attention if one is to appreciate their poetical quality and infinite variety both as regards composition and elaboration of the subject. In front of the tomb, which is indicated by a tall gravestone, the dead man sits (or stands) (fig. 45). His relatives, generally women, approach the tomb. They come to adorn it with ribbons, to place *lekythoi* on the steps, to crown it with garlands of flowers and anoint it with myrrh. Generally speaking, the scene cannot be interpreted in terms of actual events. It is an artistic creation which combines various elements of inner spiritual meaning: the dead man, his tomb, his relatives, the attention paid to the maintenance of the sepulchre. The perfect cohesion of these various elements creates an inspiring image filled with emotional content and profound grief. Over it all reigns a kind of occult silence. In front of the mourning relations rises the image of the young man taken in his prime, a handsome virile youth, carrying long spears and a round shield, his broad-brimmed felt hat thrown back over his shoulder. He rejoices in his sadness as he watches them tending his tomb; for he is aware that their mission is a token of the fact that he will always remain alive in their memory. Sometimes, exhausted by the long journey through the land of shadows, he rests on the steps of his own gravestone. In one of the later *lekythoi* the youth's intense weariness and grief, if not despair, seems to have broken his spirit. In this *lekythos,* the work of the "Reed painter", as well as in those belonging to the same group (fig. 46), the form of the human figure has lost its solid substance. But the new sense of awareness in which the figure seems to have been immersed, provides it with an unquestionably enchanting quality. The youth is "so saturated in light that his heart itself is visible". He cries out for the world he has lost. But as we too mourn beside him, we too may experience the "extraordinary passion" that fills the spirit with a strange elation as it soars into the rarefied and ethereal atmosphere of pure art. "From afar, bells of crystal can be heard ringing", as the poet O. Elytis says.

The different kinds of Greek sculpture

The National Archaeological Museum, which possesses the greatest masterpieces of ancient sculpture, is the only museum in the world to cover the whole range of ancient Greek sculpture without a single break in historical continuity. In order that the reader may follow the detailed descriptions of the sculptures in the National Archaeological Museum with greater facility he may, at this point, find a few introductory remarks of some use.

The first monumental sculptures were executed in Greece in about the mid-7th century B.C. From then on, until the last days of antiquity, innumerable sculptured works were executed in stone and metal. Soon marble, which is both abundant and of the highest quality in Greece, became the favourite material of sculptors. In about the mid-6th century B.C. two Samian artists, Rhoikos and Theodoros, invented the technique of executing hollow bronze works. Statues of bronze began to vie with those of marble, and, with the passage of time, marble and bronze took precedence over all other materials in the Greek sculptor's workshop. In Greece marble statues were painted all over: not with the natural flesh tints of the human body, but with deep bright colours — red, blue, yellow, etc. A vivid chromatic harmony reflecting the rays of the Mediterranean sun was thus created.

Sculpture in Greece was dedicated to the service of religion and the state, and it was only after the 4th century B.C. that sculptured works devorced from the affairs of the social community as a whole made their appearance. Free-standing statues and reliefs, which may be classified in two main categories — votive and funerary — had been executed by the earliest Greek sculptors. Votive sculptures depicted gods or men, and were presented as offerings in holy sanctuaries. The cult statues of gods and goddesses, which were placed within the temple, belong to this category. The funerary sculptures, which were raised on tombs, depicted the image of the dead, whose memory was thus enshrined in the minds of the living, and assumed the function of memorials. A separate group consists of the architectural sculptures which decorated the pediments, friezes and metopes of temples, as well as the *akroteria* placed on the apices of the pediments.

The fact that the so-called Daidalic style reached its zenith in the mid-7th century B.C., i.e. the age in which Greek sculpture was born, cannot be a mere coincidence. The existence of large sculptures executed in solid materials and of the emergence of the firm tectonic Daidalic style must be considered as the consequence, if not the expression, of a general and profound social and cultural differentiation. After the introduction of Oriental influences at the beginning of the century and the consequent enrichment of Greek art, it seemed dialectically imperative to follow some new direction, whereby it would be possible to synthesize the old with the new, to submit the vague and undisciplined trends of post-Geometric and "anti-Geometric" art to the laws of symmetry and balance of form. "The Daidalic style carried with it a conscious arrangement of nature, a subjection to a norm inherent in its very self". The Daidalic prelude in Greek sculpture produced a longing for grandeur and sobriety; it provided evidence of a sense of pride in the projection of conscious self-abnegation. The Daidalic sculptor certainly admired the imposing dimensions of his works, but he also knew how to subject these dimensions to a new geometric arrangement invigorated by the vital force with which forms were imbued in the ferment of the first half of the 7th century.

The first important example of this sculpture is the statue presented as a votive offering by the Naxian Nikandra at Delos in *c*. 660 B.C.: a work that contained the seeds that would eventually produce the beautiful Korai, executed both in Athens and the islands, during the period of full maturity of Archaic art; ultimately, it would also lead, through a long process of development, to the creation of the supreme masterpieces of the Classical period. The Naxian work possessed all the internal still inhibited energy that was capable of fertilizing the achievements of later years. In the context of the 7th century B.C., it was enough that it should possess a firm structure, that it should be disciplined to the closed geometric form, that there should be no breaking up of the surface of the volumes, and that there should be a total absence of any picturesque details and disruptive elements in the overall image.

The Mycenae relief, the work of an artist of a later generation, represents a figure tugging at an *epiblema* (a kind of shawl) with the right hand. No previous work possesses such complete geometric clarity or conveys such a powerful sense of interior life as that reflected in the taut stretched quality of the flesh of the head. The same feeling of tension is also apparent in the rendering of the eyes, nostrils, mouth and chin. It is the moment when the bow is drawn back to the farthest possible point, ready to hurl the arrow at the target.

Archaic Kouroi

The Cycladic statue and the Peloponnesian relief, exhibited in the first hall of sculptures, serve as curtain-raisers to the statuary's art of the Archaic period when the Greeks reserved their most maturely evolved and thoroughly integrated conception of sculpture for the creation of the figure of the Kouros, the nude "man-boy". The image of the young man was placed in sanctuaries; it was an *agalma,* dedicated to the god for his own delight, a depiction either of the god himself or of the donor who presented the statue as a votive offering. Similar figures were raised on tombs not as an ephemeral reflection of a particular incident, of a passing moment in the life of the dead youth, but as a memorial to his strength and beauty. The famous series of Kouroi in the National Museum begins in 620 B.C. with the Dipylon head (fig. 48), so-called because of the locality in which it was found. From it stems the long line of Attic Kouroi which came to an end a hundred years later in the statue of the youth Aristodikos. In the Dipylon head the pure and severe oval of the face is dominated by two large almond-shaped eyes below the arched eyebrows; the broad smooth surfaces of the cheeks terminate in the *helices* of the beautifully stylized ears; the locks of hair in the form of countless strings of beads are ranged above and below the ears.

The colossal Sounion Kouros is of a slightly later date. It is the best preserved of the four Kouroi raised as votive offerings in the temple of Poseidon on the southernmost headland of Attica. As the entire body has been preserved one is able to appreciate the firm architectural quality of the execution. While the statue retains the clear geometrical form, the sculptural volumes of the body have acquired a more pronounced differentiation, which provides both the outlines and details with greater animation. The "dormant motion" as it was first described and called by the Greek art historian, Constantine A. Romaios, is clearly discernible in this Kouros. Although all Archaic figures stand frontally, presenting the clearest and most developed image of the human body, they all seem to possess an invisible, a "dormant" though conscious sense of movement. As a result of this inner mobility the body, no longer subject to the severe axial line, acquires numerous small asymmetrical features, all of which derive from the same source and all ultimately lead, one way or another, to the same goal: the actual and positive animation of the figure. This observation and its theoretical development has provided the study of Archaic art with the means of interpreting it in terms of the most profound aesthetic appreciation and of penetrating its secrets in the most objective manner.

We are now confronted with two Kouroi, representative of the mature period of Archaic art and executed some fifty years after the Sounion Kouros, in the mid-6th century B.C. The Kouros of Volomandra (fig. 49), an outstanding work executed by an Attic sculptor, has acquired an air of spirituality and incomparable nobility. The oblong head — notice the oblique eyes, the flame-shaped locks of hair harmoniously yet loosely arranged across the forehead, the fine nose and the smiling lips — rests on a neck whose curves incline gently towards the shoulders. Animated by the reflection of a deep interior life, the Volomandra Kouros is indeed a unique work of art, a uniform as well as manifold composition. The Kouros of Melos continues the old tradition of the Naxian workshop. The soft slender body is sensitively modelled and the dignity of the hair style almost exaggerated, while the fluently traced contours follow one another in continuous curves. The youth seems to dwell in a world contemporary to but different from his Attic counterpart.

The series of Archaic Kouroi is completed by two Attic masterpieces, both funerary monuments, found at Anavyssos. The first (fig. 50) should be dated to *c.* 525 B.C. The following epigram is inscribed on the base:

> "Stand and mourn by the tomb of dead Kroisos,
> whom furious Ares snatched from among the warriors
> of the front rank."

There is a new strength in the Kouros' attitude. All the members of the body have gained in fulness and vigour. Kroisos is no longer a "man-boy"; he is a man. An unprecedented interior dynamic force gives the surface of the flesh a closely-knit aspect vibrating with vitality. The face with the tense and at the same time balanced sinuosities, the broad build of the body, the stricter arrangement of the volumes and structural forces, combine to create an image of a young man of the late Archaic period who possesses a more mature conscience, a richer experience of life, the self-confidence of a virile man in his own strength, a pride born of reasoned judgement, and a sense of humble submission to human fate.

The second Anavyssos Kouros (fig. 51), whose name, we learn from the inscription on the base, is Aristodikos, represents the last stage in the development of Archaic sculpture in Attica. The statue is also the last chapter in the history of Archaic art and of the 6th century B.C. But while closing one door, it opens another in order to usher in the art of the next century. Ernst Buschor, the German art historian, describes it as "the termination and culmination of all the Kouroi". The youth's attitude, characterized by extreme tension and the constriction of all the forces at his command, is that of someone standing on the "razor's edge". He is like a chord stretched to breaking-point; and when the chord breaks we know that its echo will resound for a long time to come. Never before has there been such a striking demonstration of the co-existence of the three successive stages in the representation of the human attitude. It is not only the tension of the youth's body which is so characteristic of the composition. The freedom and ease with which the taut attitude is reproduced are even more striking. The spirit has tamed matter and completely transformed the substance of the marble into a submissive form with ontological depth and weight. Aristodikos possesses the nobility of a man who is no longer the victim of fate; he stands fearlessly in the full light of the sun, with the dignity of a thinking man conscious of the tragic responsibilities of freedom. He is the personification of the responsible citizen of the newly-born democracy. All these diverse elements combine to find their most mature expression in this last representation of an Attic Kouros.

The Piraeus Apollo

The bronze statue of Apollo, discovered at Piraeus in 1959, is unique in many respects (it is now in the Piraeus Archaeological Museum). The oldest of bronze statues, it is the only Archaic one to have survived. It is also the oldest image of the god in monumental sculpture and the only outstanding Archaic work which clearly distinguishes the divine nature of a god from that of a mortal. The differentiation is achieved by means of the attitude of the figure and the attributes held in both hands: a *phiale* in the right, a *bow* in the left. Similarities between the Apollo and the Kouroi are of a purely superficial nature. The initiated scholar and attentive onlooker will observe that the figure is endowed with a new structural and architectural concept of the body which in itself is an expression of a completely different spiritual world. The bent elbows and the different position of the forearms (the palm of the right hand open, the fingers of the left clenched) are note mere inconsistencies, superficial variations of the established form of the rigid vertical line of the arms, but they are organically linked to the modelling and attitude of the whole body. It is easier to realise the underlying significance of the particular attitude of the figure if one bears in mind that the god, in all hieratic dignity, the weight of his body resting on both feet, is extending his right hand, in which he holds the *phiale* for the libation, inclining and slightly turning his head, in order that his gaze, filled with an expression of intense spirituality, should remain fixed on the focal point. The fact that the right leg is only very slightly advanced forward is in complete accord with the artist's conception of the figure and has no connection with the projection of the left leg forward common to the Kouroi. Modelled with unusual sobriety, the god, in full control of all his spiritual, intellectual and physical powers, turns inward on himself; his introspection exceeds the bounds of all terrestrial and corporeal existence. Without discarding his divine nature, he appears before mortals in a splendid Olympian epiphany. That such a vision of god-like grandeur and Apollonian radiance could only have been conceived and executed with such penetrating wisdom by an Athenian artist does not seem, in my opinion, to be beyond the bounds of probability. It would be also difficult to deny that this god basically expresses the genuine religious faith associated with the mature Archaic period in the course of which the magnificent pediment of the Peisistratidai was raised on the Athenian Acropolis (525 B.C.).

The Poseidon of Artemission

A striking contrast to the radiant young Apollo will be found in the formidable figure of the Poseidon of Artemision (460 B.C.) (fig. 58). There is little in common between him and the youthful god, who, with all the penitence of a libation-bearer, consorts with mortals in a mood of serene introspection. The epiphany of the mature deity is rendered with tremendous power. In his right hand, the god holds the trident, chief attribute of the mighty lord of the earth and sea, who "watches over earth and makes her shake". The trident is indeed just about to be cast. It is precisely this movement which gives the statue its main structural basis and, as it were, epitomizes the fundamental nature of the god. The modelling of the entire statue, together with all the forces that derive from it, depend on this movement of the right arm. The elevation of the arm has the effect of organically shifting the whole force of the body backwards (this explains why the toes of the left foot are raised), and of transmitting and concentrating all the tension on the right foot, the toes of which support the whole body; the constriction of the right shoulder-blade pulls back the muscles of the right side and chest which, together with the stomach muscles, are thus fully stretched. At the same time the pronounced emphasis on the great horizontal axis of the two arms counterbalances effectively all the vertical and oblique axial lines. The broad-chested body is crowned by a magnificent head; and the face, with its wide hairless surfaces, the harmoniously arranged locks of the wavy hair and beard, has an expression of supremely self-assured composure. The indomitable stength of the figure reflects the serene effortlessness and awesome grandeur of the god's inner being.

In the early Classical period repeated attempts were made to capture the essence of god-head and render it in terms of sculpture. The sculptor of the Poseidon is also believed to have executed a statue of Apollo in bronze soon after completing his magnificent depiction of the "Earth-shaker". The statue no longer survives, but an excellent Roman copy of the 2nd century A.D., known as the "Apollo of the Omphalos" (it was found along with a marble navel-stone), has been preserved. The statue, executed in deliberate *contraposto,* was notable for its free austerity and the firm yet sensitive modelling of the volumes. It was a representation of that kind of introspective god which was so much admired in an age when men's attitude to life was above all a spiritual and intellectual one. Archaeologists ascribe the original work to Kalamis, a celebrated sculptor of the mid-5th century B.C.

We would have been fortunate indeed, if any of Pheidias' statues depicting deities had survived. It appears that this greatest of Athenian sculptors had succeeded in endowing his divine figures with incomparable grandeur and profound spirituality. Advancing beyond the Aischylean conception of divinity, he reached a concept of Olympian beauty and immortality, equal to the enlightened vision of Sophokles, the poet who became the first priest of Asklepios in Athens and was heroized after his death under the characteristic name of Dexion. The diminutive marble Varvakeion Athena is but a poor reproduction of Pheidias' magnificent statue of Athena Parthenos in the Parthenon. Possibly useful for archaeological observation, it cannot attract the visitor's attention, any more than the various copies after Pheidias' works (assembled in one of the Museum halls) can replace the masterpieces now lost to us.

4th century B.C. bronze statues

The depiction of the nude male figure favoured by Greek sculptors from the earliest times reached its apogee in the Classical works of Pheidias and Polykleitos. The subject continued to be a great favourite with the sculptors of the 4th century B.C. who laid the foundations of Hellenistic art. Praxiteles, Skopas, Lysippos, each in his own way, presented an image of men and gods in conformity with the transformation of Greek society and the new ideas current at the time. In addition to these masters, many other artists, less famous perhaps, but no less worthy of note, created a number of attractive works which have been preserved.

The attitude of the human body established by Polykleitos in his superb Doryphoros (the Spear-bearer), which came to be known as "the canon"

(= Norm) had been a landmark in the history of art. By placing the weight of the body on one leg, Polykleitos stressed the flex of the other at the knee and then pulled it back. The carefully calculated rhythmical turning movements and *contraposto* provided by this form of support for the body brought new life into the depiction of the human form. All the representations of the human figure which followed Polykleitos' creations derived from this established norm. It was certainly varied and enriched, the roles of the relaxed and standing legs reversed, and one leg placed either more or less to the side; but sculptors never deviated from the basic principles of a "canon" which possessed so many potentialities. Fortunately two bronze statues have survived intact; we are thus in a position to appreciate the sculptural achievements of a century as advanced as the 4th B.C. and to distinguish the profound differences that exist between the new creations and the archetypes of Polykleitos. One of the statues, which was found in the sea near Antikythera, belonged to a consignment of works that suffered shipwreck in ancient times. The Ephebe of Antikythera (fig. 68), as the statue is now known, depicts an alert, agile and athletic young man. The well-built body is lithe and fully developed, the face expressive. The right arm is thrust forward, thus placing movement in a third dimension and cautiously opening up new horizons for some of the more daring sculptors of the Hellenistic period. Archaeologists believe an apple may originally have been held in the bent fingers of the extended right hand and that the figure might therefore have been a representation of Paris in the famous judgement scene with the three goddesses. In these circumstances, the work could be identified as the Paris of Euphranor, a renowned Corinthian sculptor of the second half of the 4th century B.C. Whether he is Paris or just some ordinary athlete, it is nevertheless interesting to note that the youth's expression and facial features, which possess a far more human and personal quality, seem to reflect a world devoid of the solid structure and inner cohesion of his 5th century B.C. antecedents.

The child-like, gentle and fragile figure of a boy, found in the sea in the bay of Marathon (figs. 71-72), is a more attractive work. The delicate modelling, the fluidity of the contours, the S-shaped movement of the spine, by means of which the figure acquires an unusual suppleness and a kind of undulating effect, possess an almost Praxitelean quality. But the new proportions in relation to head and body, deprive the figure of stability, while increasing its agility. The boy's right arm is somewhat shyly raised and his left forearm is thrust forward as though it were shearing lightly through space.

Sculptured female figures

Even the earliest Greek sculptors had not confined themselves exclusively to carving figures of nude men. But the women represented in their statues were always fully and elegantly clothed in *peplos, chiton* and *himation.* The lavish drapery remained an inexhaustible source of inspiration and plastic invention, which was not only intended to represent feminine stylishness and coquetry but to reflect the nature and interior world of womanhood. The female head crowned by a skilful arrangement of the hair or some form of head-gear, would reflect all the radiance of feminine beauty, whether it were that of an innocent virgin or a mature woman. The National Archaeological Museum does not possess a great number of large freestanding female statues. That is why the recent acquisition of a superb Archaic Kore, found together with a Kouros at Merenda in Attica, is such a fortunate event. A fine epigram with the girl's name, Phrasikleia, is preserved on the base. In addition to Phrasikleia we have a small Kore from Piraeus (height: 67 cm.), possibly a representation of Persephone, which is an original example of Attic sculpture of the Classical period (420 B.C.). The severe well-balanced attitude and freshness apparent in the elaboration of the extremely delicate folds of the *chiton* and more ponderous *himation* recall the work of Agorakritos, Pheidias' favourite pupil, who executed a large number of sculptures in Attica after his master's death.

Unfortunately only the head of a statue of a woman, which must have been an admirable example of sculpture in about the mid-4th century B.C., is preserved. In this highly praised work, known as the head of Hygeia (fig. 67), we find a remarkable synthesis of all the sculptural trends and achievements observed in statues of women executed in the mature period of the 4th century B.C. The sculptor's technical skill in the execution of the facial details is beyond praise; and his inspired conception is fully matched by the structure of the head and the rendering of the most delicate inflections and movements. Complete agreement does not exist among archaeologists whether the head does in fact represent Hygeia. Nor are they in accord as to the identity of the sculptor. Some discern the technique of Praxiteles in the limpid extremely sensitive modelling; others detect the fire and interior passion of his Parian contemporary, Skopas. It is worth noting, however, that art in the age when the work was produced had assimilated the achievements of both these masters.

Two bronze statues of female deities, which were found together with the Piraeus Apollo, are of considerable value — like all rare originals of Greek antiquity. The goddesses represented are Athena and Artemis (it is now in the Piraeus Archaeological Museum). Almost contemporary with two other bronze statues in the National Archaeological Museum, the Ephebe of Antikythera and the Boy of Marathon, the representations of the two female deities provide us with a very clear picture of the creativity of original Greek art and of the wide experience acquired by the sculptor in bronze. At the same time, both statues also reveal a flaccidity which is evident in both the structure and the treatment of plastic surfaces. It is as though the statues themselves mirrored the instability of the world in which their creators dwelt. Even more strikingly than their male counterparts, the figures of the two goddesses betray signs of the deterioration suffered in terms of form, of the attempt to replace inner dynamic force and genuine inspiration by a kind of external aestheticism coupled with an air of fictitious god-like serenity. We consequently find it somewhat difficult to agree with that expert on Classical art, K. Schefold, who suggests that the Athena may be the work of Kephisodotos, Praxiteles' father, executed at an advanced stage in his career.

During the early years of the 3rd century B.C. all the progressive trends which owed so much to the great forerunners, of whom Skopas was one, and to the more daring innovators, such as Lysippos and Leochares, came to a temporary halt. An attempt was made to revive the now vanished austerity of the old Classical tradition and to contain the figure within a severe and noble framework; the result was merely the execution of a number of well-set up but coldly decorous figures incapable of transmitting the message of the times. The statue of Themis, in the temple of Rhamnous in Attica, for instance, depicted by Chairestratos in a high-waisted garment and executed in such a way that the emphasis was strongly laid on the relaxed leg (fig. 76), may have been a perfectly agreeable work but it possessed little genuine artistic merit. The *Herakleotis* (Woman of Herculaneum) type, dated to the transitional period between the 4th and 3rd centuries B.C. is, thanks to the feeling of complete abandonment to nostalgia for the past, more attractive and elegant. The type proved to be very popular during succeeding centuries and was repeated with almost wearisome monotony throughout the Hellenistic era and, to an even greater extent during the Roman period.

Reliefs

Before examining the various sculptural forms and trends peculiar to Hellenistic art, we must once more span the whole range of Greek art in the context of the second great category of sculptures; namely, the reliefs. Although equal in quality to the free-standing statues, they greatly exceed them in quantity. If the Greeks succeeded in rendering the form of god and man in their ontological completeness by free-standing sculptures, the technique of sculpture in relief provided them with an opportunity to represent their presence in the world.

In the statues the various elements that contribute to the representation of the divine or the human essence are concentrated and self-sufficient; in the reliefs man's or god's existence unfolds in every moment of action or is depicted during a specific and variable moment of "becoming". From the beginning, the Greeks were aware of this profoundly important difference. They were thus able to endow the sculptural relief with the special character to which it was obviously most effectively suited and, at the same time, to reveal another aspect of man and the world he lives in. That is why it would be a mistake to conclude that the reliefs are a mere technical variation of the same theme.

Pedimental sculptures

There are two categories of sculptural relief: architectural groups and single pieces. Of the second category there are again two subdivisions: funerary and votive reliefs. The architectural sculptures which embellished the buildings of ancient Greece with matchless works of art were executed by outstanding artists who did not hesitate to try out the most daring innovations. Among the architectural sculptures, those adorning the pediments of temples occupy an important place in the history of art. Set at the highest point of the temple, and usually possessing considerable depth, pedimental sculptures were executed in very high relief in order that they might be properly viewed and appreciated by the onlooker below. Sculptors consequently resorted to the use of increasingly higher relief. Finally the reliefs themselves were replaced by statues sculptured in the round, although they were never seen as such. The sculptor, like the onlooker, invariably saw the figures on the pediment, with backs attached —at least, optically— to the tympanum of the pediment which possessed the same function as that of the flat surface of the plaque on which the other type of reliefs were carved. Pedimental sculptures do not therefore consist of groups or assemblies of statues carved in the round and placed at the highest point of the temple, but of compositions conceived and executed in obedience to the fundamental principles of sculpture in relief. Free-standing ornamental sculptures placed as *akroteria* on the three apices of the pediment were executed, as a rule, on the same principles.

Remains of the pedimental compositions and *akroteria* from two important 4th century B.C. temples, now in the National Archaeological Museum, give us a good idea of the artistic trends prevailing at the time no longer in isolated (and not necessarily representational) works, but in boldly inspired sculptural groups which effectively breathed new life into old themes and whose creators resorted to the most daring innovations. An entire hall is filled with the pedimental sculptures and some *akroteria* from the temple of Asklepios at Epidauros. We know that they are the work of four sculptors, two of whom were Timotheos and Hectoridas. We also know that Timotheos was an Athenian, probably an apprentice in the work-shop of Agorakritos. The *Amazonomachia* (battle of the Amazons) of the west pediment is outstanding for the dramatic quality of its composition, for its striking groupings of figures, its astonishing innovations in relation to modes of expression, and its echoes of remote mythological events. It is yet another contribution made by the Attic workshop whose creative influence extended beyond the boundaries of Athens itself. Beside the fragmentary figures of the pedimental sculptures are the charming equestrian Nereids, Aurai and Nikai (from the *akroteria)* with their light, dignified and elegant movements (fig. 65). These works seem to advance the achievements of 5th century B.C. sculpture another step forward, without in any way effecting the precise decorative function they were originally intended to fulfil.

From Epidauros Timotheos went to Halikarnassos, where he worked on the Mausoleum, the greatest monument of the century. There he must have met Skopas, one of the most inspired sculptors of the age, who is generally believed to have been responsible for some of the sculptural reliefs carved on the Mausoleum. The only sculptures which can be ascribed with any degree of certainty to Skopas, however, are those of the pediments of the temple of Athena Alea at Tegea, where he worked on his return from Halikarnassos, decorating the west pediment with a representation of the battle between Telephos and Achilles and the east with that of the Hunt of the Kalydonian Boar. The only surviving fragments of the pedimental figures now displayed in the National Archaeological Museum are the boar itself and a few heads which are animated by a feeling of deep passion and interior strength. In the following words, Sir John Beazley has not only given these sculptures the importance due to them as works of art, but also appreciated their historical significance. "The massive heads with their thickish features and the fury in their deepset eyes are the opposite of everything Praxitelean, and remind us that there was another kind of Greek left besides the cultivated Athenian —especially in Arcadia. Such were not all but most of the men who fought against the Macedonian and for him, who swarmed over the east and north, and who brought not only Greek culture, but Greek valour and resolution, wherever they went."

Attic gravestones of the Archaic period

The funerary monuments executed in relief play a very important role in the history of Greek art. Closely linked with the life of the ancient Greeks, they clearly reflect the changes which occurred in the social structure and intellectual and spiritual attitudes of the people. The National Archaeological Museum possesses a prolific collection of funerary reliefs ranging from the early Archaic age to the end of the Hellenistic period, and beyond, to the late Roman times. The collection consists of reliefs from almost every part of Greece, and in particular from Attica, where the tradition continued almost unbroken. It was the Attic model of funerary relief, too, that was finally adopted throughout the rest of the Hellenic world.

The history of the gravestones is a long one, and its origins lie in the Prehistoric period. The function of a simple stone plaque raised on a tomb was to serve as a "sign" or marker — in modern parlance, one might almost say to serve as a "signpost". Evidence of this function rests in the Greek word "σῆμα" (a sign, marker). Plaques of this kind have been found in tombs of the Middle Helladic period. The gravestones raised on the royal shaft graves at Mycenae possessed a more striking character. They had in fact acquired a monumental aspect. After the end of the Mycenaean age and the subsequent period of decline we find small undecorated plaques set up on tombs, whose position they served to indicate. But in the 7th century B.C. two very important features were added to the gravestones: an inscription with the name of the deceased and a representation of his figure. Although they first appeared separately, both features served the same end. Originally there would be a simple inscription with the name of the deceased. This simple plaque thus became the bearer of a more concrete message. It indicated not only the position of the tomb, but also who was buried in it. The representation of the figure of the deceased transformed the "sign" into a "memorial". Henceforward the funerary monument was to acquire a special character of its own both in the history of art and the social history of ancient Greece.

In the early Archaic period the gravestone consisted of a tall oblong fairly thick shaft terminating in a capital, surmounted by a sphinx, the daemon guardian of both the tomb and the deceased. On the face of the shaft, the deceased, generally a youth, would be depicted in low relief striking a characteristically manly pose as an athlete or hoplite. He was generally naked and often held a weapon identifying him as an hoplite. As a rule he was depicted advancing to the right. An image of aristocratic sobriety, he stood alone on his memorial, "ideal in his grief" as the poet Cavafy says. His youthful vigour and beauty were invariably idealised. Sometimes a brief epigram described his origins and the cause of his death. Not a few of these were genuine sculptural masterpieces executed by the most able sculptors. A precious fragment of one of these the incomparable head of the Discophoros (the discus-bearer) (fig. 53), dated to c. 550 B.C., was no doubt the work of the sculptor who executed the "Peplos Kore" and the Rampin Horseman of the Athenian Acropolis. The gravestone of Aristion (fig. 55), in which the figure of a hoplite is carved with a remarkable feeling for plasticity, is the work of Aristokles, a sculptor whose name is known from other works executed by him in the one but last decade of the 6th century B.C. The gravestone of the "Running Hoplite" (fig. 54), unique in both its shape and representation, is a work of such delicate modelling, such elegant conception, that if it was not executed by Antenor himself, the outstanding sculptor of the late Archaic period, it must surely be attributed to some member of his workshop.

Gravestones from other parts of Greece

During the first half of the 5th century B.C. no further gravestone were raised in Attica: probably as a result of some proscriptive law passed by Kleisthenes. But the tradition was preserved in other parts of Greece, and the works executed by non-Attic sculptors were not without artistic merit. The shape of the shafts remained basically the same, but there was a decisive change in the representation of the figure carved in relief. The shaft no longer showed a young athlete or hoplite — lone, dignified and invariably handsome. Men of mature age, leaning on a staff as they turned to play with their faithful dog at their feet, are represented in a whole series of gravestones executed in the islands. The gravestone of Alxenor is a good example of this category, and the inscription eloquently describes its significance and the pride the sculptor felt in his work, when we read, "Alxenor the Naxian made me. Admire me". The subject of another shaft of a very slightly later date is unique. A provincial work, of Akarnanian provenance, devoid of the finished workmanship associated with other Greek sculptures, it nevertheless indicates the extent to which the influence exercised by the great art centres had spread. Again the deceased is represented as a man of mature years; a *himation* thrown over his shoulder, his head raised, he plays on a lyre which he holds in his left hand. The young man represented in a later gravestone, found at Larisa, has a less sophisticated air; he is more rooted to his fertile Thessalian soil. The drapery of a woollen garment falls in heavy folds and a *petasos* covers his head. In his right hand he holds a hare, in his left a fruit. Nothing could be more striking than the difference between this peasant of a remote province and the elegant citizens of Athens or the active landowners of Attica who breathed the stimulating air of the great capital. The same difference is observed in the buxom women of the countryside, clad in austere dowdy garments, like the figure represented on the gravestone of Polyxenaia and the slightly more elegant figure on the gravestone of Amphotto which came respectively from Larisa and Boiotia. Recalling the supremely distinguished maidens of the Cyclades, immortalised in the gravestones displayed in other museums, one realises the extent to which their grace and beauty must have been inspired by their environment, by the cool breezes and foam-crested waves of the Aegean. Any kind of comparison between them and their cumbersome graceless sisters of the mainland would indeed be a cruel one.

Attic funerary reliefs of the Classical period

Gravestones began to be raised again in Attica in the mid-5th century B.C. — or, possibly, a little later. But they now seem to belong to another world. Both the form of the shaft and the subject matter of the relief have undergone a radical change. The shaft is no longer a tall oblong plaque with the representation of the single figure of the deceased, but has lost height, while gaining in width. As a logical sequence of this transformation its finial has assumed the shape of a pediment instead of a palmette. Figures of women now appear beside those of men, and the deceased is no longer always depicted standing: he is sometimes seated. The deceased is accompanied by a second person, standing opposite him. This person frequently extends his hand towards the deceased in a gesture of greeting — *dexiosis* the ancient Greeks called it. The gesture most probably expresses the feeling that the living are still attached to the dead person and that this attachment has not been wholly severed by the reality of death. With the passage of time, more figures are represented on the shaft; an entire family may even be seen accompanying the dead person. There is more variety in the representation of the deceased. Not only age but also social and professional status, even the actual cause of death, may be indicated or hinted at. But the deceased always preserves an air of other-worldly dignity, and his (or her) serenity is not devoid of a trace of regret for the lost world of the living.

From the purely plastic point of view, it is possible to follow the gradual process through which the figures became almost detached from the plaque. At the time of the construction of the Parthenon (430 B.C.) figures carved in relief were attached to the plaque, as the figure's thickness was minimal. Gradually, however, figures acquired an entity of their own as they were carved in increasingly high relief, until before the mid-4th century B.C. the plaque had assumed the aspect of a separate body against which the volumes of the figure, now carved almost in the round, were projected.

While this decisive change in the sculptural form of the gravestones was taking place, the representation of the deceased was also being transformed into that of an "individual character". At first it was a kind of distant faraway expression, or even the actual attitude of the figure, that indicated the person to be the deceased. Later the face acquired an other-worldly air; the eyes no longer met those of the other persons; the gaze went far beyond, as though fixed on some remote and infinite void. In about the middle of the 4th century B.C. the figure appears to become increasingly isolated; sometimes it acquires a special glow and on occasion, it reaches the point of a "heroic" isolation.

Wandering through the hall of the Classical gravestones one is soon conscious of the fact that these curiously withdrawn figures emanate an atmosphere of strange beauty — the kind of beauty which is difficult to disassociate from the grief caused by death — and of a feeling of serenity akin to the attainment of eternity. In the Salamis gravestone (fig. 61), the young man who holds a bird in one hand seems to belong to the rarefied atmosphere of the Parthenon sculptures. He is a blood-brother of the handsome young riders of Pheidias' frieze. Some sculptor who worked on the frieze, probably a Parian, must surely have carved the face of the Salamis youth on the marble plaque. The body, though liberated and independent, gives the impression of being subject to an interior spiritual discipline.

It would not be an exaggeration to say that no gravestones achieved such classical balance and "celestial beauty" as that of the Salamis youth, had not the gravestone of Hegeso, which is of slightly later date, survived intact (fig. 62). "In the lines of the design, in the feeling of animation produced by the sculptured surface and in the attitudes of the two figures..." writes Christos Karouzos, "one finds a rare distinction and evident nobility. The longer one looks at this work, the more one inclines to the belief that not a single line in the design, not a single detail of the attitude of the body and arms can be changed, even to the most infinitesimal degree, without effecting a radical alteration of the whole work. One might go so far as to say that the spirit of human nobility had achieved its final and definitive form in this work."

The fact that these two works may be set apart as supreme masterpieces of Attic art does not mean that other gravestones are not of the highest quality. They are all evidence that Classical art in Athens not only attained supreme heights but also expanded and embraced the whole of the social community. The spiritual wealth of the Athenians and the remarkable sensitivity of Athenian artists (both as regards conception and execution) are clearly reflected in the variety of representations carved on the gravestones. At random, let us take those of Ktesileos and Theano, or the one from Piraeus in which the deceased and her servant girl are depicted, or again those of Mnesarete, of Prokles and Prokleides, and of Polyxene. They all present a different picture of the same disturbing theme, a new interpretation of the eternal tragedy of death. The series which began with two supreme masterpieces (the Salamis youth and Hegeso) may be said to come to an end with two equally fine works of the last decades of the 4th century B.C., the gravestones of Ilissos (fig. 63) and of Aristonautes (fig. 64). Many archaeologists detect the hand of Skopas in the former. We have now come, as we have already observed, to the highest spiritual level, and the young in the gravestone of Ilissos has reached complete isolation, while his aged father gazes at him with an expression of profound sorrow, his little serving boy crouches at his feet and his dog sniffs at the ground. The young man's state of complete nudity, which permits the sculptor to give a perfect finish to his body, together with the youth's expression and attitude, combine to raise the figure to "heroized" stature. In the gravestone of Aristonautes the deceased hoplite, depicted all alone against the deep background of a temple-shaped edifice, advances impetuously across the uneven ground. Sorrowfully he seems to watch some passer by — or perhaps only gazing into infinity, "beyond this earth and men" (G. Seferis). With the close of the 4th century B.C. the history of Attic gravestones comes to an end. Once again a law, this time passed by Demetrios Phalereus (317-307 B.C.), proscribed the raising funerary monuments. Assuming different forms, they were now confined to modest little columns, insignificant shafts or works remarkable only for their ostentation and pomposity.

Votive reliefs

The second category of single pieces of relief sculpture consists of the votive ones; and there is a large collection of these ranging from the early Classical to the late Hellenistic periods in the National Archaeological Museum. The upper part of a gravestone found at Sounion shows a young athlete crowning himself (fig. 60). The shaft, which depicted a nude youth, is a striking example of Attic sculpture of the severe style, and it foreshadows the figures of the Parthenon frieze. The "Melos discus" on which the head of Aphrodite is depicted in profile is absolutely unique. The profile of the goddess is the work (dated to 460 B.C.) of a great Parian sculptor who, combining an extraordinarily sensitive execution of the curves with a delicately carved relief, succeeded in conveying the essence of exquisite feminity.

But the most impressive of all the votive sculptures of the Classical period is the large Eleusinian relief in which Demeter is depicted presenting Triptolemos with the precious ears of corn, while Persephone crowns him (fig. 59). The majesty of the figures, their god-like austerity and the profound religious quality of the scene are superbly rendered. The conception underlying the composition of the relief, the nobility and fullness of the lines and volumes, the perfect harmony of the folds of drapery are a revelation of what Attic artists were capable of accomplishing in Classical times, in the age of the Parthenon.

A votive offering sculptured on both sides dedicated to Hermes and the Nymphs, which was found at Neon Phaleron, once the deme of Echelidai, where the hippodrome of ancient Athens lay, is dated to the late 5th century B.C. On one side it shows the pair of heroes, Echelos and Basile, riding a chariot, in front of which stands Hermes himself (fig. 66). On the other side are representations of Artemis, Kephisos, horned in the manner of river gods, and three Nymphs. The work is notable for the liveliness and grace of the figures and its superb sculptural finish.

The curtain comes down on the 5th century B.C. with the Peloponnesian War. Disease, destruction and slaughter were now the lot of the Greeks. The great gods of antiquity no longer possessed the attributes required to offer solace to a people faced with so many problems. Men's hearts began to warm increasingly to Asklepios, a forgotten provincial deity, a simple healer and philanthropist. First at Epidauros, then in Athens and other parts of the Hellenic world, the sanctuaries of Asklepios were crowded with worshippers in search of medical treatment. The fame of Asklepios' miraculous "healing remedies", soon spread throughout the country and his faithful worshippers presented him with countless votive offerings. A hall in the National Archaeological Museum is entirely filled with reliefs from the Athenian Asklepieion which was situated on the southern slope of the Acropolis. The god is generally depicted leaning on a stick, accompanied by two of his daughters, Hygeia and Iaso, and sometimes also by others like Akeso and Panakeia, whose names have a clearly therapeutic connotation. The worshippers, bearing offerings of animals or fruits, include men and women of every social class. In one of the votive offerings a cart-driver is represented; from the inscription we learn that he was saved by the god.

Similar reliefs from the great sanctuary of Asklepios at Epidauros, displayed in another hall, provide further evidence of the power exercised in the 4th century B.C. over men's minds by the figure of this benign god and of the faith he must have inspired in all those pilgrims who flocked to his sanctuaries laden with rather costly votive offerings. The offerings of the poorer people consisted of clay objects or wooden tablets which were hung on the walls of the sanctuary buildings. Such tablets were found in the cave of Pitsa near Corinth (fig. 39) and constitute unique and consequently precious specimens of Archaic painting. An idea of what one of these sanctuaries may have looked like can be obtained in a hall in the National Archaeological Museum. In the centre stands an altar dedicated by the Athenian Boule in c. 210 B.C. to Aphrodite Hegemone and the Charites. Statuettes and reliefs of every kind and every period are placed around it. Among these are two reliefs: one of Hermes and the Nymphs dated to 460 B. C. discovered in a cave on Mt. Pentelikon; another of the late 4th century B.C. in which Hermes and the Nymphs are again depicted, accompanied this time by Pan playing on his *syrinx*. There is also a Roman relief of allegorical figures depicted in a garden which was discovered on the site of Herodes Atticus' villa at Loukou in Kynouria. The hall is furthermore filled, just like the great or small sanctuaries once were, with an enormous and confused collection of statuettes and reliefs of Pan, of Herakles, Zeus and Aphrodite.

Portraiture

All the works so far examined, including certain specific depictions of figures in the funerary sculptures, clearly reveal the artist's idealistic conception of his subject, which prevented him from rendering personal facial traits: in other words, from creating a genuine portrait. In the course of the 4th century B.C., however, one finds that certain figures go beyond the established "type" and may be considered to be representations of specific persons. The National Archaeological Museum possesses an outstanding example: the bronze boxer from Olympia (fig. 73). Without departing from the established "type", the sculptor succeeded in rendering the individual features of an actual person; more important, he managed to model the boxer's features, which possess all the coarse characteristics associated with a man of his profession, amid a mass of thick hair, beard and moustaches.

Another bronze head, known as the Philosopher of Antikythera, is an example of the outcome of this trend in the Hellenistic era (fig. 74). In this work every trace of the old idealism has vanished; the man's personal features are revealed in his face, and the modelling is executed in such a way that the flabby flesh, untidy hair and wrinkled face are all very carefully rendered. The eyes seem to reflect the man's profound and restless contemplation of the world; his lips appear to be ready to speak. The last stage of Hellenistic portraiture is represented by a remarkable bronze head of a man found at Delos (fig. 75). The longer one looks at it the better one is able to distinguish all the adventures through which Greek art had gone. The expression of the man's face epitomizes his anxieties: the uncertainty, the sense of emptiness and anguish caused by something he has lost, by something he seeks beyond this world.

Henceforward sculptured portraits become increasingly popular and during the Roman period countless portraits of emperors and high-ranking officers were executed not only in Rome itself but in every part of the far-flung empire. The National Archaeological Museum possesses an important collection of these sculptured portraits which are of considerable interest both to scholars of the Roman period and to amateurs anxious to cover the entire span of ancient sculpture.

Hellenistic sculpture

In this introductory review of the sculptural works in the National Archaeological Museum the examination of Hellenistic sculptures has been left to the end. The reason for their apparent disassociation from the rest of Greek sculpture lies in the fact that the products of the Hellenistic period cannot be included in any of the established categories and that in their great variety, which lacks definition, they reflect the countless trends, demands and requirements of the people who created them. Besides the portraits of ordinary mortals, statues of gods, now depicted on a colossal dimensional scale, continued to be executed. Among the most impressive works are the heads and other fragments of the cult statues of Despoinei, Demeter, Artemis and the giant Anytos from Lykosoura in Arkadia, executed by Damophon, a famous 2nd century B.C. sculptor, as well as the head of Zeus from Aigeira in Achaia, an admirable example of the period. Other figures of gods, such as the Poseidon of Melos (fig. 77) and the Aphrodite with Pan of Delos (fig. 78) illustrate how remote is the age when faith filled men's hearts. The pompous attitude of Poseidon and the sugary feminity of Aphrodite seem to have less in common with the deities themselves than with actors impersonating them. And just as the hearts of men are now devoid of faith so are the structure and modelling of the figures drained of their former divine force.

Hellenistic artists were not incapable, however, of creating some powerful and attractive works. The statuette depicting the figure of a little boy holding a goose (3rd century B.C.), found on the northern foothills of Mt. Parnassos in ancient Lilaia, possesses a freshness which strikes a very different note from anything seen in earlier Greek art. The boy has a charming smile, the flesh of the body is soft and tender and the air of seriousness which distinguishes the attitude of the figure is not without an attractive quality. The so-called "little refugee", which reached the National Archaeological Museum from Gerondiko near Nyssa in Asia Minor after the exodus of the Greeks in 1922, possesses the same kind of unusual charm and reflects the eternal freshness of Ionian art. Barely able to stand on its tiny feet, the child, clad in a heavy hood, clasps a dog tightly in its arms. It is not only charm, however, that characterizes Hellenistic art. The sense of power and *élan* that overwhelmed the world following the conquests of Alexander the Great is admirably reflected in the art of the period. The long voyage through Greek sculptural masterpieces is brought to a fitting conclusion by two important works: a large funerary relief and the "jockey boy" of Artemision. A horse, an animal always popular with Greek sculptors of all ages, is depicted in both sculptures. In the relief the stubborn untamable beast, which may be favourably compared with any of the noble horses depicted on the Parthenon frieze, raises its head proudly, while a young negro groom, standing in front of it, frantically tries to control it (fig. 79). We should certainly have possessed a more flattering and accurate picture of Hellenistic art, had more masterpieces of this kind survived. In the circumstances let us be thankful that the relief has been preserved, together with its bronze counterpart: the bronze horse on which the jockey boy is mounted (fig. 80) and which we are at last able to appreciate in its original completeness, as a result of the prolonged efforts made by skilful craftsmen of the National Archaeological Museum to piece it together. The youthful rider seems to be of diminutive size in relation to the enormous animal which gallops along frenziedly. The boy's face, constricted with tension, is a supreme example of realism in Hellenistic art, comparable only to the striking modelling of the horse's body and head. The unique skill displayed in the modelling of the head actually induced Ernst Buschor, a very highly esteemed scholar in Greek sculpture, to suggest that the work was one of the 5th century B.C. and place it next to the archetypal figures of the Pheidian horses. In actual fact, however, it has been established beyond doubt that the whole composition, including horse and boy, which were recovered from the sea off Cape Artemision together with the great bronze Poseidon, is a work of the Hellenistic "baroque" period of the 2nd century B.C.

Metal works. The minor arts

The National Archaeological Museum possesses a very fine collection of small-scale works in bronze. The most important is the Karapanos collection which consisted basically of bronze objects of the minor arts from the area of

Dodone, although it also included works of exceptional craftsmanship from other parts of Greece. It is not easy for the modern observer to assess the true significance of the bronze works of art executed in ancient Greece owing to the fact that the greater part of the large bronzes have not been preserved and those that have indeed survived were discovered quite fortuitously, as in the case of the Piraeus statue; others, it will be remembered, were hauled up in fishermen's nets from ancient shipwrecks. The bronze objects of the minor arts thus help us to fill in the picture we have formed from an examination of the monumental sculptures. They furthermore enable us to realise that the high quality of both technique and artistic expression was not limited solely to monumental sculpture but extended to all levels of creative art throughout the Hellenic world. Many of these bronze objects, such as the rider from Dodone (fig. 84), were presented as votive offerings in sanctuaries by pious worshippers who did not possess the financial means to commission lavish statues. Some of these works, such as the weapons, cuirasses, helmets, tripods, mirrors etc., possess a functional purpose; others formed part of the decoration of the above objects, as, for instance, the small Geometric horses, griffins and numerous small idols. The production of these objects during all periods ranging from Geometric times to late antiquity provides evidence of the sculptural skill of the Greeks even in those early times when large sculpture was as yet unknown. At the same time, the artistic form of these objects, which kept strictly in step with the continuous transformations of large sculpture, enables us assuredly to consider them as a part of the whole artistic spectrum and, consequently, to appreciate them as such.

The head of Zeus from Olympia (fig. 86), which must have formed part of some small statue of the god, is representative of the most mature achievements of Archaic art in the beginning of the 5th century B.C. A small head of a youth from the Athenian Acropolis (fig. 87), which is of a slightly later date and perhaps came from a Peloponnesian workshop, reflects the profound spiritual quality of the art of the Severe Style. The Geometric horses, which either adorned the rim or handle of cauldrons or stood alone on a separate base constitute the earliest examples of Greek sculpture (fig. 81). Their clear form and firm structure foreshadow the basic principles on which Hellenic sculpture was to develop. The Oriental origin of the griffins' heads, which adorned the rims of cauldrons (fig. 82), indicates the foreign influences to which Greek art was subject in the early 7th century B.C. The awe with which the greatest of the Olympian deities must have filled the hearts of pious worshippers is revealed in the numerous bronze idols of Zeus represented in the act of preparing to cast his thunderbolt (fig. 83). These idols were the first attempts made by craftsmen to depict the figure of the god at the moment of his mighty supremacy. The idols of Athena Promachos (fig. 85) provide a parallel image of a deity depicted in all her martial spirit, a spear held in her raised right hand, a shield in her left, always ready to champion the cause of the beloved Athens.

Jewellery

The gold objects in the Mycenaean collection provide sufficient evidence of the fact that the goldsmith's craft was practised in Greece from the earliest times. The execution of superb ornaments wrought in metals (particularly gold) and precious stones, continued in the historical era. The National Archaeological Museum always possessed some exquisite specimens of this craft ranging over all the periods; but a recent donation made by Helen Stathatos has further enriched it with a collection of the most rare and remarkable objects. The show-cases contain every kind of precious ornament: necklaces, bracelets, earrings, pins, diadems, funerary crowns and a quantity of other objects which reveal the unique skill and sensitivity of the Greek goldsmiths. Among the most rare and unusual objects is the remarkable medallion with a female bust carved in relief, framed by a fine and delicately worked chain, which is a genuine masterpiece of the minor arts. Then there is a magnificent relief carved in gold in the shape of a little temple (fig. 89), in which the figure of a drunken Dionysos is represented supported by a Satyr. The base and pediment, studded with small polychrome stones, is superbly executed. The object's function remains a mystery. But whether it was costly votive gift offered to the deity of some sanctuary or a mere ornament in the house of some wealthy Greek family, it provides us with another reminder — as indeed all the other objects in the collection also do — of the wealth owned by the citizens of Greece and of their impeccable taste and refined way of life (figs. 90-91).

The Numismatic Museum

The point may now have been reached when the visitor to the National Archaeological Museum, having examined such a vast variety of collections, feels a sense of surfeit. Nevertheless this review of the priceless treasures here would not be complete without reference to the Numismatic Museum (figs. 92-95). The first Greek coins appear to have been struck in the 7th century B.C. From the outset coinage played a special role — different from that of any other object in the minor arts — for the very reason that some characteristic symbolical representations were stamped on the circular surface of the coins of each different city. We thus have representations of deities or figures with daemon-like natures, of local fruits and animals, of symbolic depictions of place names, such as a rose *(ρόδο)* for Rhodes, an Apple *(μῆλο)* for Melos, etc. Finally, after the Classical period, we get portraits of kings. As Charles Seltman, the numismatist, has said, the Greeks possessed an irrepressible impulse to decorate every object of common use with the utmost good taste. They thus created the finest coins in the world, executed by famous craftsmen who had acquired all the experience required for working on precious metals and stones. And as the Greek city states were in the habit of frequently changing their coinage — with the notable exception of Athens — we are able to follow the stylistic development of forms — frequently in all its unbroken continuity — in a whole series of coins. An examination of the Numismatic Museum thus completes the picture of Greek art, as we originally conceived it, in the form of a journey, taken step by step, in all its various stages and all its different manifestations, from the dawn of prehistory to the twilight years of the ancient world.

1. Stone idol from the area of Sparta. The corpulent female figure, with prominent buttocks, breasts and stomach, is a typical example of a work of the very earliest phase of the Neolithic Age (6000-5000 B.C.).

3

4

2. Clay figurine of Kourotrophos (nursing mother), found at Sesklo. She is depicted enthroned and richly adorned. End of the Neolithic period.

3. Vase from Dimeni. Admirable works, in which the elegant shape of the vase vies with the well-conceived intricate decoration, were produced by Thessalian potters in the last phase of the Neolithic Age.

4. Vase from Lianokladi. The skill of the potters of the earlier Neolithic Age is evident in this spherical vase with its remarkable outlines and simple yet striking decoration.

5. *Marble idol of a harpist from Keros. The firmness of the architectural structure of the figure and the intricate harmony of the curves of the volumes developed within the space in which the work is confined combine to create a unique sculptural entity. 2800-2200 B.C.*

6. *Marble idol of a flute-player from Keros. Contemporary to the idol of the harpist and of equally high quality, the work provides evidence of the skill of Cycladic artists in rendering the human figure in different and unusual attitudes. 2800-2200 B.C.*

7. *Large marble statue of a female figure from Amorgos. The primitive creator of this masterpiece of Cycladic sculpture (2800-2200 B.C.) achieves a plastic rendering of the female form by means of delicate undulating lines. The sculptural work was complemented by paint applied to the mouth, eyes and other facial features.*

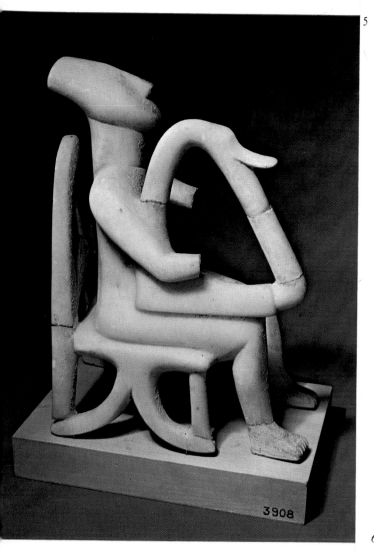

5

6

8. *Clay object in the shape of a frying-pan from Syros, with incised decoration of tangent spirals among which a ship is depicted. A very characteristic example of a large group of similar objects whose function remains unkown. 2800-2200 B.C.*

9. *Stone utensil with lid from Naxos. The artist's skill in working on stone contributes to the creation of a genuine minor work of art of great elegance. 2800-2200 B.C.*

8

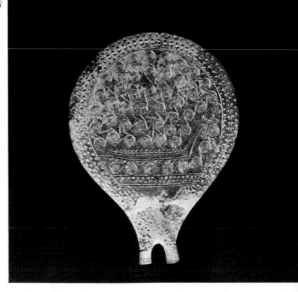

9

45

10. The fresco of the Boxing Children from a house at Thera. Two children engage in a boxing game with an air of disarming seriousness. They wear boxing gloves (this is the earliest known representation of boxing gloves). The faultless rendering of the bodies and their movements reveal a very considerable knowledge of a child's anatomy. c. 1550 B.C.

11. The fresco of the Fisherman. One of the best preserved frescoes from the so-called West House at Thera depicted two fishermen, one of whom (height: slightly more than one metre) is almost wholly undamaged. Unique in Minoan art, the fisherman is represented nude. In both hands he holds his catch of fish (mackerel), the mouths of which are hooked to a piece of string.

12. *Fresco of the Antelopes, two of which are depicted here. The composition consisted of six similar animals. The originality shown in the sketching of the animal's outlines by means of alternately wide and narrow brush strokes, the sinuous curve of the contours and the rendering of the heads and legs of the animals reveal the high artistic level attained by the artist and his thorough knowledge of his subject-matter. Provenance: Thera.*

13. *The fresco from the House of the Ladies, in which a representation of a group of three women was found, gives us an idea of the elegance and intricacy of the clothes worn by Minoan women. The 'lady' in this fresco is depicted advancing to the left; her movements are lively, and she extends her arms forward. She may have been making an offering to a female deity. Provenance: Thera.*

12

13

14. The fresco of the Spring. Fragment of an enchanting fresco depicting a rocky site overgrown with bright red lilies. Pairs of swallows fly overhead in pursuit of their erotic games, as though intoxicated by the air of spring and the flower-scented earth. The composition is most probably associated with the performance of some spring rite. Provenance: Thera.

14

17

15. *Rhomboidal gold sheet with seven lance-shaped laminae found in Grave III of Grave Cirle A at the acropolis of Mycenae. It must have crowned the head of the young woman buried in the grave. 16th century B.C.*

16. *Vessel of rock-crystal in the shape of a duck. The finish given to the work is of outstanding quality. The rendering of the bird's neck and head and the exceptional delicacy of the carving of the curved line raise the object to the level of a masterpiece of sculpture in stone. Found in Grave O of Grave Circle B at Mycenae. 16th century B.C.*

17. *Gold funerary mask which Schliemann believed to be that of Agamemnon.It is the most characteristic of the masks found at Mycenae, and the facial features of the Achaian king buried in Grave V of Grave Cirle A are rendered very realistically. 16th century B.C.*

18, 19. *The two gold cups with decoration in embossed relief have been found in a tholos tomb at Vapheio in Lakonia. The capture of a bull in a net, which has been spread between two trees, is depicted on one cup, an idyllic scene with cattle on the other. 15th century B.C.*

20. *Silver rhyton in the shape of a bull's head. The horns and rosette on the forehead are of gold. This magnificent example of the Mycenaean goldsmith's art is comparable to the rhyta, also in the shape of bull's heads, of Minoan Crete. Found in Grave IV of Grave Circle A at the acropolis of Mycenae. 16th century B.C.*

20

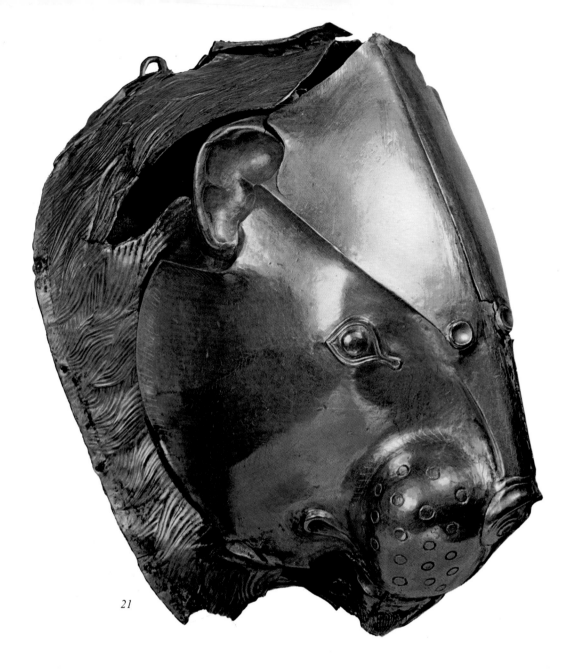

21

21. *Gold rhyton in the shape of a lion's head. It comes from Grave IV of Grave Circle A at the acropolis of Mycenae (16th century B.C.).*

22-24. *Elaborate bronze daggers with inlaid ornamentation of gold, niello and amber. They were found in Graves IV and V of Grave Circle A at Mycenae. 16th century B.C.*

25. *Gold sword-handle (length: 0.24 m.). This is the largest of all preserved Mycenaean sword-handles. Found in a Mycenaean grave (1500 B.C.) on the island of Scopelos.*

26. *Bronze dagger with elaborate gold handle inlaid with cyanus and rock-crystal in a combination of the* cloisonné *and* à jour *techniques. Found in Grave IV of Grave Cirle A at the acropolis of Mycenae. 16th century B.C.*

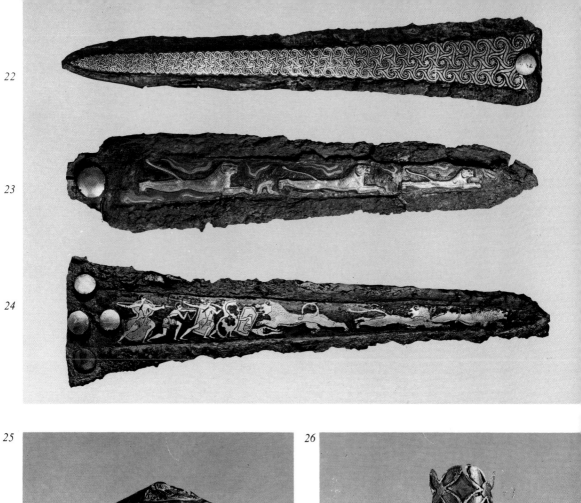

22

23

24

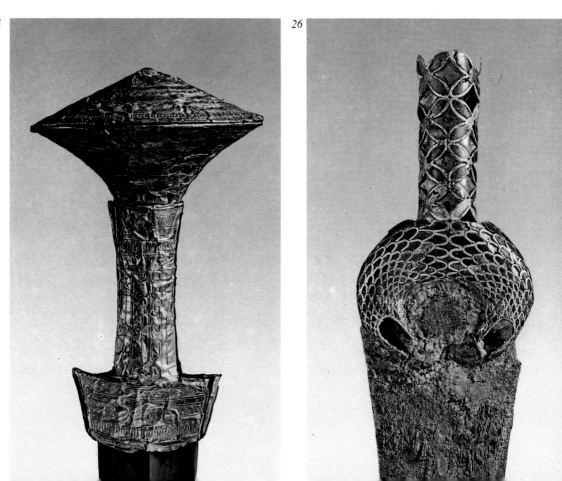

25

26

27. Ivory head of a warrior carved in relief. The warrior wears the usual Mycenaean helmet, the exterior of which was reinforced with boar's tusks. It comes from a chamber tomb of the lower city of Mycenae. 13th century B.C.

28. Masterpiece of Mycenaean minor sculpture in ivory. Two women are depicted embracing each other. One of them holds an infant in her arms. The identity of the persons depicted in the group remains an enigma. It has been suggested — somewhat rashly, perhaps — that the group is a very early representation of Demeter, Persephone and the young god, Iakchos. The belief that it was a representation with a religious significance is supported by the fact that it was found in the area of the repository of the sanctuary of Mycenae. 13th century B.C.

29. Rare specimen of Mycenaean sculpture. Limestome head of a woman whose features are not only rendered plastically, but also painted with bright colours. It was found in a house south of Grave Circle A at the acropolis of Mycenae. 13th century B.C.

30. *The famous Warrior Vase, in the shape of a krater, is unique in Mycenaean vase-painting. Mycenaean hoplites are depicted marching in phalanx (probably on their way to battle). Behind them a female figure raises one hand in a gesture of farewell. The subject-matter and character of the figures· are wholly Mycenaean, devoid of any Minoan influences. One might say that the work is a remote ancestor of 7th century B.C. Greek vase-painting. The krater was found in a house south of Grave Circle A at the acropolis of Mycenae. c. 1200 B.C.*

31. *Fragment of a fresco, labelled the Mycenaean Woman, found in 1970 by Professor G. Mylonas in a house built within the west wall of the Mycenaean acropolis. It is the finest example of Mycenaean painting known to us. The firm design, the lavish colours and, above all, the originality shown in the rendering of the dignified figure are unique in Creto-Mycenaean painting. Dated to the last years of the 13th century B.C.*

31

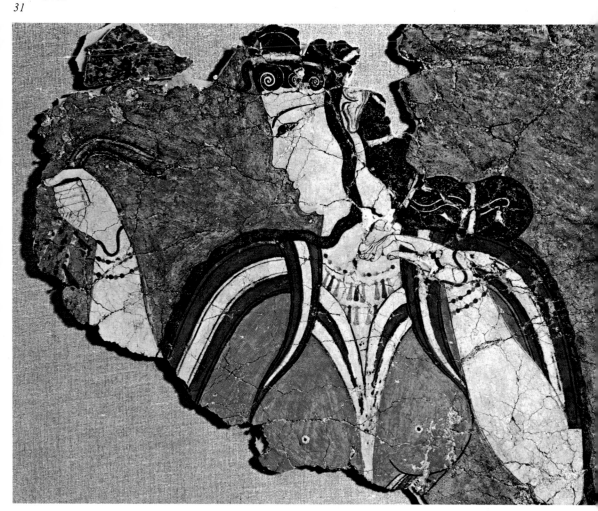

32. *Monumental Geometric amphora from the Dipylon Gate of the Kerameikos. The architecture and general organisation of the parts are faultlessly executed. The decoration is both lavish and a perfect expression of Geometric art. The prothesis (lying-in-state of the dead) is depicted in a band between the handles. 760-750 B.C.*

33. *Monumental krater from the Dipylon Gate of the Kerameikos. Like the amphora reproduced in fig. 32, it was placed on a tomb as a funerary monument. Geometric decoration is strictly restricted. The carrying out of the corpse to burial on a carriage, followed by the deceased's friends and relations, is depicted on the main band, a procession of chariots on the lower one. 740 B.C.*

34. *Amphora from Melos. The representation on the neck shows two warriors in combat. A suit of armour is depicted between them. On either side stand two female figures, possibly the mothers of the combatants. Apollo is represented mounted on a chariot drawn by winged horses on the body of the vase. He holds the kithara with seven strings in his left hand and the plektron in his right. He is greeted by Artemis, who stands in front of the chariot, leading a stag by her right hand and holding a bow in her left hand. 625-620 B.C.*

32

33

34

35

35. *The Nessos amphora, found at the Dipylon Gate of the Kerameikos, is one of the earliest black-figure vases. The combat between Herakles and the Centaur Nessos is depicted on the neck. The body is decorated with a representation of the legend of Medusa's decapitation by Perseus. 620 B.C.*

36, 37, 38. *Sculptured vases in which human faces are depicted. The fact that Athenian vase-painters created a large number of similar works in the late 6th and early 5th century B.C. provides indisputable evidence of the great influence exercised by large sculpture over the artists who worked at the Kerameikos.*

39. *Wooden votive tablet found, together with other similar ones, in the cave of Pitsa, near Corinth. A rare specimen of Greek painting in the Archaic period (540 B.C.), it represents a sacrificial scene. To the right is the altar which the worshippers approach with their offerings. A small boy leads the sacrificial animal (a lamb). All the participants are crowned with garlands in accordance with ritual ceremony.*

36, 37, 38

39

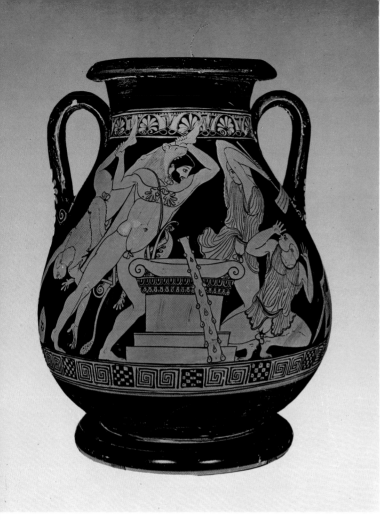

40

41

40. *Red-figure pelike, the work of the so-called 'Pan painter', decorated with a depiction of the tragic-comic episode in which Herakles slays Bousiris. Superb specimen of the period of the severe style. 470 B.C.*

41. *Red-figure calyx krater, the work of the so-called 'Syriskos painter'. On one side Theseus is represented with the Minotaur in the Labyrinth; on the other, the sons of Pandion, king of Attica, Pallas, Nisos and Lykos (brothers of Aegeus) and the son of Erechtheus, Orneus. 470 B.C.*

42. *Red-figure stamnos, the work of the vase-painter Polygnotos, whose creations are assigned to around 425 B.C. A young man, holding two javelins, pursues a female figure.*

43. *Panathenaic amphora. On the front side an inscription records the name of the archon Kallimedes (360/59 B.C.).*

44. *The epinetron of Eretria. This curious product of the potter's craft was worn by women on their thigh (the fore part was adjusted to the knee) for spinning wool. The epinetron shown here is ascribed to the so-called 'Eretria painter' (c. 425 B.C.). Alkestis is depicted in her bridal chamber, while her sister-in-law, Hippolyte, plays with a bird. The work is one of the most elegant examples of red-figure vase-painting of the late 5th century B.C.*

45. White-ground lekythos. In front of the funerary stele, the tall base of which consists of six steps, stands a young spearman wearing a chlamys. Lekythoi and garlands are placed on the steps. The mound itself is visible behind the stele. The young man is dead. Time and space have no reality in the white-ground lekythoi; all is confused in a kind of other-wordly unity. The work is by the so-called 'Bosanquet painter'. c. 440 B.C.

46. White-ground lekythos found at Eretria. The dead man, depicted as a warrior, wearing a chlamys, sits wearily on the base of the stele, using the two upright spears beside him as support. A woman and a young man flank the central figure of the deceased who dominates the scene. The freely and easily drawn line of the design succeeds in conveying the sense of weariness felt by the dead warrior who finds himself alone and abandoned in a realm beyond the terrestrial world he knows. The work is one of the last in the series of white-ground lekythoi of the late 5th century B.C. and is ascribed to the 'R' group associated with a masterly vase-painter, the so-called 'Reedpainter'.

47. White-ground lekythos bearing the representation of a female figure (not apparent in the plate), Charon and Hermes. The work is by the so-called 'Sabouroff painter', one of the outstanding vase-painters of white-ground lekythoi, and a contemporary of Pheidias.

46

47

67

48. *The Dipylon Head, which formed part of a statue of the earliest Attic Kouros (620-610 B.C.). The severe geometric shape, the wide forehead and bead-shaped locks of hair provide the work with an austere charm.*

49. *Funerary Kouros known as the Kouros of Volomandra. The work is representative of the mature phase of 6th century B.C. Attic sculpture.*

50. *Funerary Kouros. The statue was found at Anavyssos in Attica. 525 B.C.*

51. *Funerary Kouros, whose name, as recorded by the inscription on the base, was Aristodikos. The work is the last in the series of great Attic Kouroi and the terminal point reached by Archaic sculptors. 500 B.C.*

48

49

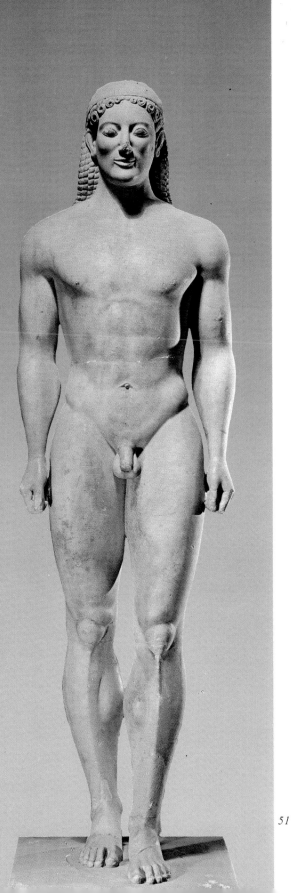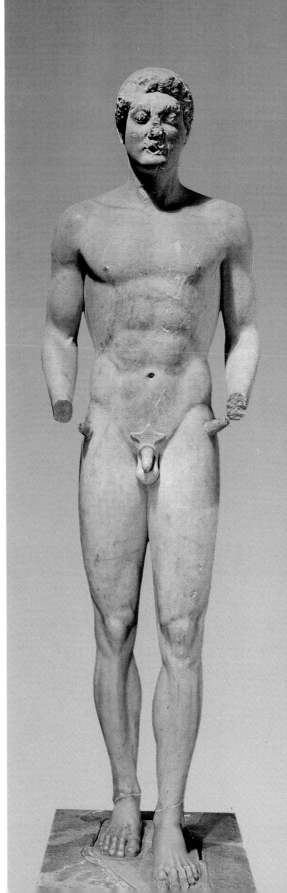

51

52. Detail (head) of the Kouros in fig. 50, identified by an inscription on its base as 'Kroisos'.

53. The Diskophoros Head. Part of an Archaic gravestone of the mid-6th century B.C. In his raised left hand the young athlete holds the discus which is discernible behind his head. The work is ascribed to the sculptor of the Rampin Horseman in the Acropolis Museum.

54. The stele of the Running Hoplite. An unusual work depicting a nude helmeted young man in the act of running. The work must have formed part of a funerary monument and was probably surmounted by a palmette. 510 B.C.

55. The stele of Aristion, 'the work of Aristokles' as recorded by the inscription on the base; one of the best preserved Attic stelai of the Archaic period. It must have been crowned by a palmette. The dead man is depicted as a warrior. 510 B.C.

53

54

55

56. *Base of an Archaic statue of a Kouros, found built into the Themistoklean wall (478 B.C.). Representations of young athletes are carved in relief on three sides. On the side reproduced in fig. 56 six athletes are depicted playing a ball game in teams of three each. The low relief carving set against a painted red ground gives the work a charming pictorial quality. 500 B.C.*

57. *Base of a statue found, like the one reproduced in fig. 56, built into the Themistoklean wall. Again the base is carved with representations in relief on three sides. On the side depicted in fig. 57 is a procession of chariots and hoplites. This work, too, was executed in low relief and the ground was painted red. 490 B.C.*

58. *The Poseidon of Artemision. This magnificent bronze statue was found at the bottom of the sea-bed near Cape Artemision, Northern Euboia. The arm was first discovered in 1926, and the rest of the statue in 1928. The god is represented at the moment when he raises his right arm with tremendous force in order to hurl the trident against an adversary (some archaeologists believe the representation to be one of Zeus about to cast a thunderbolt). The plastic rendering of the god's body, depicted in an attitude of extreme tension, and the forceful expression of the face combine to create a matchless masterpiece, executed in bronze during the last years of the severe style. 460-450 B.C.*

56

57

59. *The great Eleusian votive relief offered by some wealthy initiate in the Mysteries. To the left, Demeter holds her divine sceptre in her raised left hand; in her right hand she holds the ears of corn which she is about to present to Triptolemos, the young king of Eleusis. The nude youth strikes a heroic attitude as he stands in front of the goddess and respectfully raises his right hand to receive the precious gift. Behind him, to the right, stands Kore (Persephone), holding her divine attribute, a tall taper, and raises her right hand to crown the young hero, fully conscious that he is worthy of the great mission entrusted to him. The work is a masterpiece of Attic sculpture of the Classical period. 430-420 B.C.*

60. *Votive stele found near the temple of Athena at Sounion. A nude ephebe raises his right hand to crown himself after winning a victory in an athletic contest. A particularly fine example of Attic sculpture of the early Classical period. 460-450 B.C.*

61. *Upper part of an Attic gravestone. A young man, his well-built chest bare, a himation thrown over his left shoulder, holds a bird in his left hand and raises his right arm towards a cage. A cat sits on the summit of a stele below the cage. In front of the stele stands a nude serving boy gazing mournfully before him. The spirit of great artistic creation which distinguished the supreme moment in Attic sculpture, as witnessed in the Parthenon sculptures, is reflected in this sepulchral memorial. All art historians agree that the stele must have been executed by a great artist who worked on the Parthenon sculptures.*

60

61

62. The epistyle of the pedimental finial of this much-admired gravestone bears the inscription Ἡγησὼ Προξένου (Hegeso, wife or daughter, of Proxenos). The young and dignified Hegeso is seated on a beautifully-wrought chair with back. 410 B.C.

63. The stele of Ilisos. To the left a young man, almost entirely nude, leans against a stele with a two-tiered base, holding a lagobolon (club for flinging at hares). To the right stands an elderly man resting his chin on the palm of his right hand and staring at the young man, surely his son, with an expression of grief. The work is an outstanding example of the last phase of Attic gravestones. The melancholy isolation of the young man cannot be anything less than an expression of the creative genius of a great sculptor of the 4th century B.C. — possibly, in the opinion of some scholars, Skopas. 340 B.C.

64. A funerary temple-shaped little edifice, the memorial of Aristonautes. The unknown sculptor, inspired by his dramatic subject-matter, has succeeded in achieving a total expression of the pain of death and of the complete isolation of the deceased. The figure's violent movement beyond the confines of the temple-shaped edifice seems to surpass the limits of space as conceived by Classical artists. 320-310 B.C.

62

63

65

66

65. Akroterion from the temple of Asklepios at Epidauros. A female figure — a Nereid or Aura — is seated on a horse which is probably in the act of emerging from the sea. 380 B.C.

66. Votive relief carved on both sides. On the side reproduced here the hero Echelos is depicted in the act of abducting the heroine Basile. On the uneven ground in front of the four-horse chariot stands Hermes. The plaque was found at Neon Phaleron near the deme of Echelidai where the hippodrome of ancient Athens lay. c. 400 B.C.

67. The head of Hygeia, generally considered to be one of the finest in the whole of Greek sculpture. The deep 'interior life', which seems to emanate through this work, has led some art historians to conclude that the head is a creation of Skopas. On the other hand, the flowing and exquisite modelling of the flesh surfaces has led others to classify it among the early works of Praxiteles. 350-340 B.C.

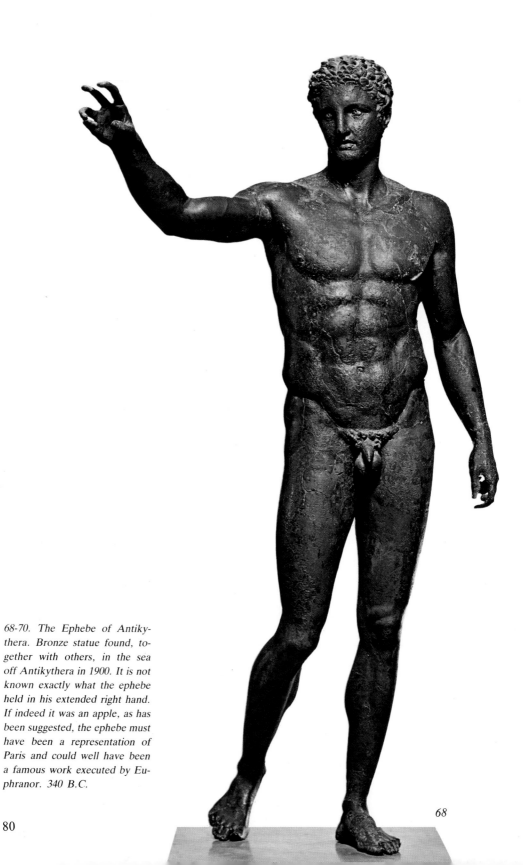

*68-70. The Ephebe of Antiky-
thera. Bronze statue found, together with others, in the sea
off Antikythera in 1900. It is not
known exactly what the ephebe
held in his extended right hand.
If indeed it was an apple, as has
been suggested, the ephebe must
have been a representation of
Paris and could well have been
a famous work executed by Euphranor. 340 B.C.*

68

69

70

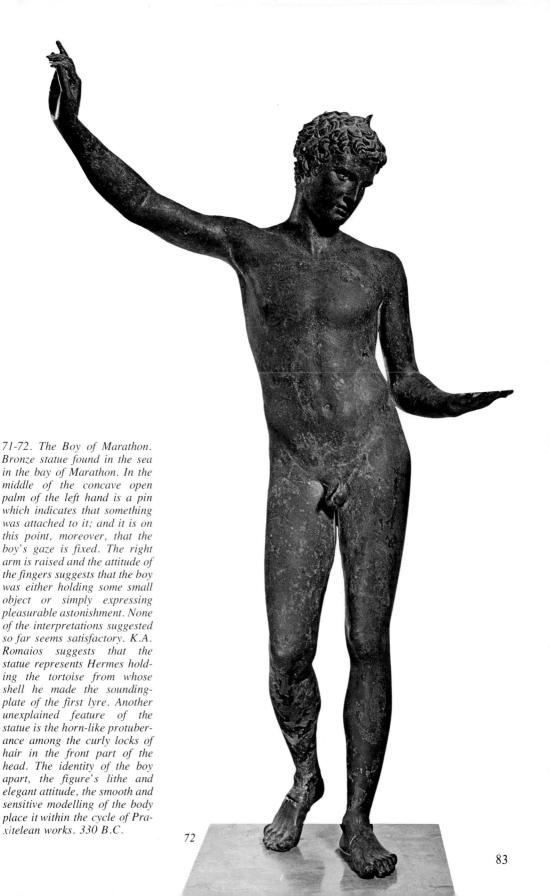

71-72. The Boy of Marathon. Bronze statue found in the sea in the bay of Marathon. In the middle of the concave open palm of the left hand is a pin which indicates that something was attached to it; and it is on this point, moreover, that the boy's gaze is fixed. The right arm is raised and the attitude of the fingers suggests that the boy was either holding some small object or simply expressing pleasurable astonishment. None of the interpretations suggested so far seems satisfactory. K.A. Romaios suggests that the statue represents Hermes holding the tortoise from whose shell he made the sounding-plate of the first lyre. Another unexplained feature of the statue is the horn-like protuberance among the curly locks of hair in the front part of the head. The identity of the boy apart, the figure's lithe and elegant attitude, the smooth and sensitive modelling of the body place it within the cycle of Praxitelean works. 330 B.C.

72

73. *Bronze head of a boxer. Part of a statue of a victor in a boxing contest, a votive offering from the sanctuary of Zeus at Olympia. The work is a portrait in the modern sense of the word. While remaining faithful to the tradition of rendering the 'type' of his model, the artist endeavours to depict the personal characteristics of a specific person. This work stands on the threshold of the long history of portraiture. The boxer in question is probably the famous athlete Satyros, and the portrait may have been executed by the well known Athenian sculptor, Silanion. 330 B.C.*

74. *Bronze head of a philosopher. Found in the sea, together with the bronze ephebe, at Antikythera. The rendering of the individual features of a specific person is self-evident. Comparing this work with the head reproduced in fig. 73, we may observe the extent to which the 'type' has been replaced by a more direct and personal form of actual characterization. 240 B.C.*

75. *Bronze head of a man found in the palaistra at Delos. It probably formed part of a statue of a standing male figure. The head is turned to the left, but the man's glance, directed slightly upwards, as though he were gazing into a void, reflects an interior world full of anxiety and uncertainty. The work is one of the finest sculptured portraits of the late Hellenistic period. Early 1st century B.C.*

73

74

75

76. *Statue of the goddess Themis, found in the temple at Rhamnous. In her extended right hand the goddess must have held a phiale (a kind of bowl) and in her left a pair of scales. She is clad in a chiton, high-waisted immediately below the breasts and a himation. From the inscription on the base we learn that the work, executed by Chairestratos, was presented as a votive offering by Megakles of Rhamnous. 280 B.C.*

77. *The Poseidon of Melos, found at Melos together with other marble statues, in 1877. The god's attitude has a somewhat pompous and theatrical air, an interior emptiness and ostentation which has lost the strength and warmth of feeling of authentic Hellenistic art. End of 2nd century B.C.*

78. *Group including Aphrodite and found at Delos. Pan, goat-footed, is trying to embrace the nude goddess who has removed her left sandal with which she teasingly threatens to strike him. A show of more warmth of feeling would have provided charm to a work which is, in reality, little more than a purely pictorial representation devoid of inspiration. c. 100 B.C.*

76

77

79

79. *Fine relief from a funerary monument. A fiery horse, whose body is covered with an animal-skin, raises its head violently, while a little black groom tries to control it. One of the most powerful works of the early Hellenistic period.*

80. *Horse and jockey boy of Artemision. The problem whether the horse and rider actually belong to the same composition remains unsolved. Only painstaking research on the part of art historians is likely to produce conclusive evidence. The horse is rendered in an attitude of extreme tension, both as regards the modelling of the head and the forward projection of both head and forelegs. The tremendous speed at which the horse is galloping causes the little chiton with numerous narrow folds worn by the jockey boy to be blown back. The boy's little face is constricted to the point of ugliness and his small lithe body contorted by the effort he is obliged to make. The work is a fascinating example of the human passion which artists of the peak period of the Hellenistic era succeeded to infuse into their most inspired works. Dated to about the mid-2nd century B.C.*

81

82

83

84

81. *Geometric bronze horse on a perforated base. The neck and legs are composed of laminae. c. 750 B.C.*

82. *Bronze bust of a griffin from Olympia. It formed part of the decoration attached to the rim of a cauldron. c. 750 B.C.*

83. *Bronze statuette of Zeus found in the course of excavations at Dodone. In his raised right hand, the god holds a thunderbolt which he is about to cast. c. 460 B.C.*

84. *Bronze rider from Dodone. The rider was part of the Karapanos Collection, whereas the horse was found in 1956, during excavations at Dodone. There is a similar horse, also from Dodone, in the Louvre. The rider in the Athens piece may have been mounted on the Louvre horse. The two pieces may have formed a single votive offering representing the Dioskouroi. c. 560 B.C.*

85. *Bronze idol of Athena with helmet and aegis, from the Acropolis of Athens. The goddess is represented in the Promachos type, extending her left hand in which she carried a shield and raising a spear with her right hand. c. 450 B.C.*

86. *Bronze head of Zeus from Olympia. Part of a votive statuette of the father of the gods. The eyes, which were executed in a different material and inlaid, slant obliquely below the curved eyebrows which form two perfect arches starting from the nose, thus giving the face an air of spiritual austerity. A very fine piece of work of the late Archaic period.*

87. *Bronze head of a young man from the Athenian Acropolis. Part of a statuette dedicated to Athena. The eyes were inlaid. The structure of the head is firm, the plastic modelling of the cheeks and chin severe and heavy; the eyelids, eyebrows and lips are thick. The man's expression possesses the austerity of a work associated with a Peloponnesian workshop of the period of the severe style. c. 470 B.C.*

88. *Cheek-piece of bronze helmet from Dodone. Two warriors are represented; the one standing, wearing a chlamys and helmet (or pilos) and holding a shield, gazes at his opponent whom he has overthrown. The defeated warrior is depicted kneeling on the ground. Last quarter of the 5th century B.C. Karapanos Collection.*

86

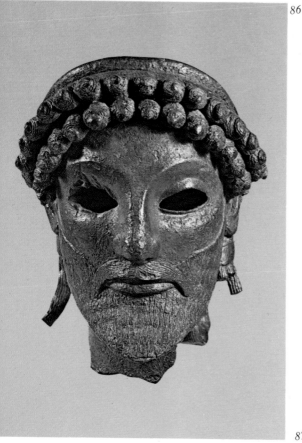

87

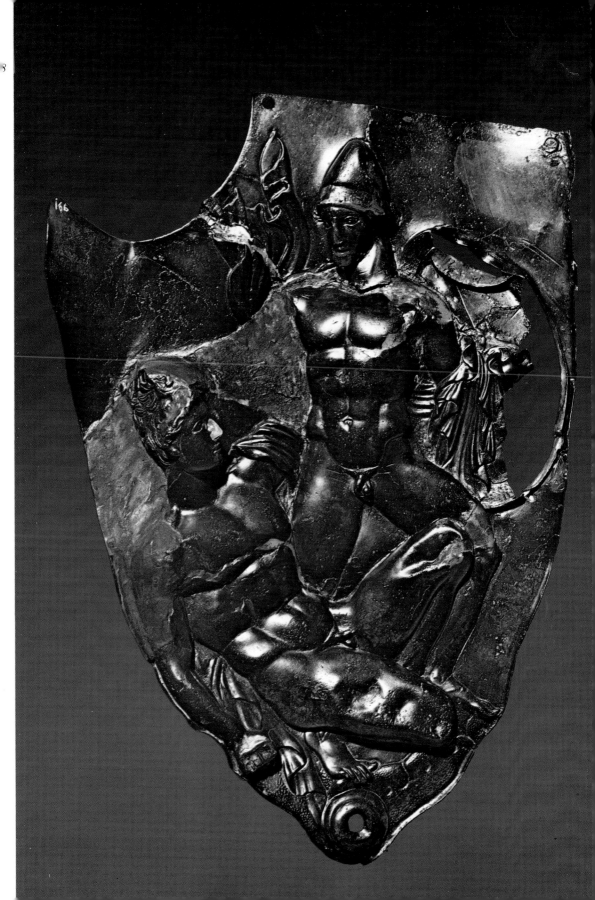

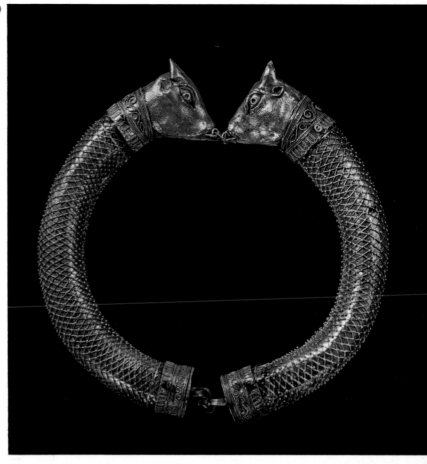

89. *Gold object in the form of a little temple. Dionysos is depicted in very high relief, flanked by a panther (left), and a Satyr (right). The god, behind whom a thyrsos is placed obliquely, wears a wide garment held by a clasp round the neck, leaving the upper part of the body bare. Dionysos, who appears to be in ecstasy, leans and supports himself on the young Satyr. Provenance: Thessaly. Dated to the late Hellenistic period. H. Stathatos Collection.*

90. *Gold bracelet, composed of two thin tubular sections covered with filigree, terminating at the upper end in bulls' heads. Possibly dated to the 3rd century B.C. Provenance: Thessaly. H. Stathatos Collection.*

91. *Two gold bracelets with double spirals, the upper parts of which terminate in snakes' heads, the lower in the reptiles' tails. Precious stones are placed in the spaces between the coils of the snake's body in one of the bracelets, which bears on the inner side the inscription ZΩILAC. Hellenistic period. Provenance: Thessaly. H. Stathatos Collection.*

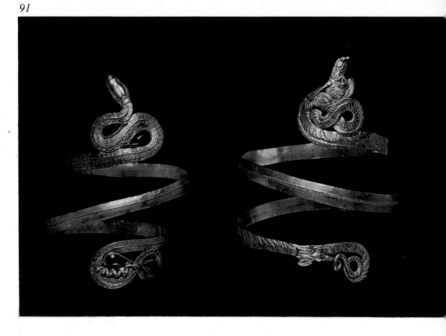

92. *Tetradrachm. Athens. 5th century B.C.*

93. *Tetradrachm. Mende. c. 425 B.C.*

94. *Gold octadrachm of Ptolemy V. Early 2nd century B.C.*

95. *Gold stater with representation of head of Titus Quinctus Flamininus. c. 196 B.C.*

92

93

94

95